CONTENTS

PAGE

For One Man

Valley Forge—*serious* . . . Maxwell Anderson . 3

Rain from Heaven—*serious* . . S. N. Behrman . . 6

Tobacco Road—*serious* . . . Jack Kirkland
from the novel by
Erskine Caldwell 7

Point Valaine—*serious* . . . Noel Coward . . . 9

Noah—*semi-serious* . . . . Andre Obey, English
text by Arthur Wil-
murt 10

Candlelight—*comedy* . . . Siegfried Geyer . . 12

The Bishop Misbehaves—*comedy* Frederick Jackson . . 13

A Murder Has Been Arranged—
melo-dramatic . . . . . Emlyn Williams . . 16

For One Woman

Dodsworth—*serious* . . . . Sinclair Lewis,
dramatized by
Sidney Howard 21

Daisy Mayme—*serious* . . . George Kelly . . . 22

Nine Till Six—*serious* . . . Aimée and
Philip Stuart 24

Mary of Scotland—*serious* . . Maxwell Anderson . 26

Accent on Youth—*comedy* . . Samson Raphaelson . 27

Lover's Leap—*comedy* . . . Philip Johnson . . 29

Mr. Faithful—*comedy, cockney* . Lord Dunsany . . . 30

No More Ladies—*comedy* . . A. E. Thomas . . . 32

CONTENTS

		PAGE
Outward Bound—*supernatural* . Sutton Vane . . .		33
Brief Candle—*romantic* . . . Robert Hare Powel		35
The Noose—*melodramatic* . . Willard Mack . .		36

FOR ONE MAN AND ONE WOMAN

Mrs. Moonlight—*fantastic* . . Benn W. Levy . .	41
Big Lake—*folk-fantasy* . . . Lynn Riggs . . .	44
For Services Rendered—*serious* . W. Somerset Maugham	47
Accent on Youth—*comedy* . . Samson Raphaelson .	50
I Love an Actress—*comedy* . . Laszlo Fodor . . .	53
Petticoat Fever—*comedy* . . . Mark Reed	55
Lady of Letters—*comedy* . . . Turner Bullock . .	58
The Bride the Sun Shines On—	
comedy . . . . Will Cotton . . .	62
Three Cornered Moon—*comedy* Gertrude Tonkonogy	65
The Curtain Rises—*comedy* . . Benjamin M. Kaye .	73
Thunder on the Left—*fantastic* . Jean Ferguson Black	
	from the novel by
	Christopher Morley .	75

TWO MEN

Laburnum Grove—*semi-serious* . J. B. Priestley . . .	81
The Wind and the Rain—*serious* Merton Hodge . . .	87
Small Miracle—*semi-serious* . . Norman Krasna . .	91
The First Legion—*dramatic* . . Emmet Lavery . .	94
On to Fortune—*satirical* . . . Lawrence Langner and	
	Armina Marshall	98
Page Miss Glory—*comedy* . . Joseph Schrank and	
	Philip Dunning	101

TWO WOMEN

The Distaff Side—*serious* . . . John Van Druten . .	107
The Joyous Season—*serious* . . Philip Barry . . .	109

SCENES FOR STUDENT ACTORS

VOLUME II

ARTHUR MILLER - ALL MY SONS
T. WILLIAMS - GLASS MENAGERIE

SCENES FOR STUDENT ACTORS

Dramatic Selections from Plays

VOLUMES I, II, III, IV, V AND VI

EDITED WITH NOTES

BY

FRANCES COSGROVE

SCENES FOR STUDENT ACTORS

Dramatic Selections from New Plays

VOLUME II

EDITED WITH NOTES

BY

FRANCES COSGROVE

SAMUEL FRENCH, INC.
45 West 25th Street   NEW YORK, N.Y. 10010
7623 Sunset Boulevard   HOLLYWOOD 90046
LONDON   *TORONTO*

TO

MY MOTHER AND FATHER

PREFACE

Since the first volume of "Scenes for Student Actors" was published, about a year ago, I have had occasion to discuss it with various teachers and students who have made practical use of the volume.

As a result of these discussions I have attempted to incorporate in "Scenes for Student Actors, Vol. II" certain suggestions that have made it more valuable both to the student and to the teacher. In the main this book was designed to meet the needs of the high school and junior college student, though I feel confident it will be useful to university and other amateur groups as well.

In this volume, as in the first, I have used selections from our contemporary theatre, including some which, though they have been produced on Broadway, have not yet been available to the amateur through publication. There are several selections from plays successfully produced in London that have not as yet reached the New York stage. I have endeavored as far as possible to assemble a variety of situations and characters and have included more scenes that rely on pantomime than in the first book. The scenes chosen are, in general, somewhat longer than those in the earlier volume, as this seemed to be one of the most common criticisms. Following another suggestion, I have included more scenes for women.

In those cases where it has been necessary to cut certain passages the omission is indicated by a series of dots.

The student will find the scenes classified in the index to enable him to choose the proper selection. A book list is appended for the use of those students who may wish to pursue the study of entire plays.

PREFACE

I wish to thank the authors and the publishers of the selections included in this book for their permission to use them. I also wish to express my appreciation of advice rendered me by Mr. Barrett H. Clark, and to Mr. Merlin P. Cosgrove.

CONTENTS

PAGE

The Old Maid—*serious* . . . Zoë Akins
from the novel by
Edith Wharton 112

The Cradle Song—*serious* . . Gregorio and Maria
Martinez Sierra,
English version by
John Garrett Under-
hill 116

The House of Connelly—*semi-
serious* . . . . . . Paul Green . . . 121

Burlesque—*comedy* . . . . George Manker Watters and Arthur
Hopkins 123

The Truth Game—*comedy* . Ivor Novello . . . 125

GROUP SCENES

Men in White—*comedy* . . . Sidney Kingsley . . 133
4 men

Nine Pine Street—*comedy* . . John Colton and
Carlton Miles 135
3 women

Nine Till Six—*semi-serious* . . Aimée and
Philip Stuart 138
3 women

FOR ONE MAN

VALLEY FORGE [1]

by

Maxwell Anderson

The scene is a bunk-house at Valley Forge. The soldiers, starving and threadbare, wish to go home for the winter. WASHINGTON *is kind but firm. He is tired but he has not yet given up. He is an inspiring figure to his men.*

WASHINGTON. Well, Master Teague, if they catch you they'll give you seventy-five lashes, and that's a good deal to take and live. On the other hand you're quite right from your own angle, and if I were you I'd feel as you do.—But this you should know, sir: if you go home, and we all go home this winter, you won't need to bother about coming back in the spring. There'll be no fighting to come back to.—General Howe will march out of Philadelphia and take over these states of ours. If he knew now how many have deserted, how many are sick, how many unfit for duty on account of the lack of food and clothes and munitions, he'd come out in force and wring our necks one by one, and the neck of our sickly little revolution along with us. So far we've kept him pinned in Philadelphia by sheer bluster and bluff and show of arms. We've raided his supplies and cut off his shipping and captured his food-trains and so bedeviled him generally that he thinks there's still an army here. But every able-bodied man, every man that owns a pair of dungarees for his legs and brogans for his feet, has to look like ten men if this nation's coming

[1] Copyright, 1934, by Maxwell Anderson. Reprinted by permission of the author and publishers.

through the winter alive.—What are we in this war for? Are we tired of it? Do we want to quit? . . . It may be you're here in error, and the sooner you discover it the better. You'll get death and taxes under one government as well as another. But I'll tell you why I'm here, and why I've hoped you were here, and why it's seemed to me worth while to stick with it while our guns rust out for lack of powder, and men die around me for lack of food and medicine and women and children sicken at home for lack of clothing and the little they need to eat—yes, while we fight one losing battle after another, and retreat to fight again another year, and yet another and another, and still lose more than we win, and yet fight on while our hair grows gray and our homes break up in our absence, and the best and youngest among us give their blood to swell spring freshets and leave their bones and marrow to flesh the hills. This is no lucky war for me. I thought it was at first. I wanted to astound the world as a military leader, but my head's grayer now and I've had enough of that. What I fight for now is a dream, a mirage, perhaps, something that's never been on this earth since men first worked it with their hands, something that's never existed and will never exist unless we can make it and put it here—the right of free-born men to govern themselves in their own way.—Now men are mostly fools, as you're well aware. They'll govern themselves like fools. There are probably more fools to the square inch in the Continental Congress than in the Continental army, and the percentage runs high in both. But we've set our teeth and trained our guns against the hereditary right of arbitrary kings, and if we win it's curfew for all the kings of the world.—It may take a long time, but one by one, bolster themselves as they will, pour out money as they may for mercenaries, make what victorious wars they can, they'll slip one by one from their thrones and go out with the great wash through this breach we make in their sea walls.—It may not be worth the doing. When you deal with a king you deal with one fool, knave, madman, or whatever he may be. When you deal with a congress you deal with a conglomerate of fools, knaves, madmen and honest legislators, all pulling different directions and shouting each other down. So far the knaves and fools seem to have it. That's why we're stranded here on this barren side-hill, leaving a bloody trail in the snow and chewing the rotten remains of sow-belly on which some merchant has made his seven profits.—So far our government's as rotten as the sow-belly it sends us. I hope and pray it will get better. But whether it gets better or worse it's your own, by God, and you can do what you please with it—and what I fight for is your right to do what you please with your government and with yourselves without benefit of kings.—It's for you to decide, Master Teague—you, and your son, and the rest of you. This is your fight more than mine. I don't know how long the Congress means to keep me where I am nor how long you mean to stay with me. If you desert they may catch you and they may not, but the chances are they won't, for the sentries are men as you are—hungry, shivering, miserable and inclined to look the other way. Make your own decision. But if we lose you—if you've lost interest in this cause of yours—we've lost our war, lost it completely, and the men we've left lying on our battle-fields died for nothing whatever—for a dream that came too early—and may never come true.

RAIN FROM HEAVEN [1]

by

S. N. Behrman

HUGO WILLENS, *a literary and music critic, is a German refugee. He is quiet, and very distinguished. He is at a houseparty just outside of London, and is talking to his hostess.*

HUGO. (*Not too seriously.*) There's no such thing as absolute friendship. Like everything else, friendship is relative —a thermometer of expediency. . . . I'm glad you can believe in friendship. It must be a great comfort to you! . . . I did once. . . . I was aware of one friend. He was an unknown playwright. I felt this man to be, though he was even then middle-aged, the freshest and the most living voice, since Ibsen, in Europe. In my first published book a large part was devoted to him. But the book brought me more success than it brought him—as a result of it I was invited to lecture in America. I took his plays with me, I translated them and lectured on them from New York to San Francisco. Now, you must understand that in all this, I was exalting myself; it was the most any critic can be, a disciple of greatness. . . . And I had the greatest reward such discipleship can have. As a result of my enthusiasm a curious phenomenon took place; the fame I created for him in America reverberated to Germany— and we began to accept him at home! . . . He's over sixty. I've hero-worshipped him for thirty years. I came to see him, sure that in his mellow greeting I would be in some sense—restored. Because I actually felt a wavering of sanity. I had sent him the manuscript of my pamphlet. I began to tell him how disturbed I was by the New Dispensation when I detected a new look in his eyes, a new manner. He had not smiled in greeting; he had not given me his hand. He refused point-blank to read my pamphlet; in a hard voice he advised me to tear it up. "This is a new day," he said to me. "There is no place in it for Oriental decadence!" Oriental! My family had lived in Germany for hundreds of years. I sat there staring at him. In his eyes, already glazed with mortality, I saw something impenetrable, incurably hostile, something that no appeal to the past could soften. That look did for me. I'd never had such a sense of helplessness. For in his youth this man had been the voice of the submerged—he had written the saga of the oppressed and the poor; he had been a living instrument of justice. There he sat, impersonal, hard, fanatical. He let me go without asking me to come to see him again, as you let go a servant who has cheated you and to whom you refuse to give a reference. . . . Friendship!

TOBACCO ROAD [1]

by

JACK KIRKLAND

From the novel by Erskine Caldwell

JEETER LESTER *lives on a small farm that has long since fallen into decay. Years of poverty and malnutrition have made their mark on* JEETER. *His clothes are old and dirty. His face is thin and unshaven. At the moment, he is trying to arouse his son-in-law's sympathy. He speaks in a monotone.*

JEETER. My children all blame me because God sees fit to make me poverty-ridden, Lov. They and their Ma is all

[1] From *Tobacco Road* by Erskine Caldwell and Jack Kirkland. Copyright, 1934, by Jack Kirkland and Erskine Caldwell. Published by The Viking Press, New York.

the time cussing me because we ain't got nothing to eat. It ain't my fault that Captain John shut down on giving us rations and snuff, and then went away and died. . . . I worked all my life for Captain John, Lov. I worked harder than any four of his niggers in the field; then the first thing I knowed he came down here one morning and says he can't be letting me get no more rations and snuff at the store. After that he sells all the mules and goes up to Augusta to live. He said there wasn't no use trying to run a farm no more—fifty plows or one plow. He told me I could stay on the land as long as I liked, but that ain't doing me no good. Ain't no work I can find to do for hire and I can't raise a crop of my own because I ain't got no mule and I ain't got no credit. That's what I'm wanting to do powerful strong right now—raise me a crop. When the winter goes and when it gets time to burn off the broom sedge in the fields, I sort of want to cry. I reckon it is the smell of that sedge smoke this time of year near about drives me crazy. Then pretty soon all the other farmers start plowing. That's what's the worst. When the smell of that new earth turning over behind the plows strikes me, I get all weak and shaky. It's my nature— burning broom sedge and plowing in the ground this time of year. I did it for near about fifty years, and my Pa and his Pa before him was the same kind of men. Us Lesters sure like to stir up the earth and make plants grow in it. The land has got a powerful hold on me, Lov. . . . It didn't always used to be like it is now, neither, Lov. I can remember a short time back when all the merchants in Fuller was tickled to give me credit. Then all of a sudden Captain John went away and pretty soon the sheriff comes and takes away near about every durn piece of goods I possessed. He took every durn thing I had, excepting that old automobile and the cow. He said the cow wasn't no good because she wouldn't take no freshening, and the automobile wasn't no good neither. I reckon he was right, too, because the automobile won't run no more and the cow died.

POINT VALAINE[1]

by

NOEL COWARD

MARTIN WELFORD *is an English aviator. He is a young, sensitive boy. Due to a crash in the jungle he has come to Point Valaine, an island in the British West Indies, to convalesce. He is a bit weak, now, from an attack of fever. He is talking to the proprietress of the hotel.*

MARTIN. I didn't crash. I had to make a forced landing because the damn fool mechanic hadn't put in enough petrol. I pancaked onto the trees. . . . That means shutting off your engine and dropping, as slowly and gently as you can. . . . I hardly damaged the plane at all. . . . Then we climbed out and got down into the jungle. . . . I had a mechanic with me. . . . I was, [entirely alone] after a little while. . . . He went mad and hanged himself with his belt. I'd left him in a clearing for a few hours, because I thought we were near the main river where I could get help. But it wasn't the main river at all, and when I got back I found him like that, hanging from a tree. It was quite a low tree, his feet were only a few inches from the ground. That was on the sixth day. . . . I went on. There wasn't anything else to do. . . . [I ate] Roots mostly, and leaves. I used to try to catch animals at night, but I never succeeded. . . . We started with a revolver, and we took the compass out of the plane too, but we lost them both in the first river we crossed. . . . I got to within

[1] From *Point Valaine*, a play in three acts, by Noel Coward. Copyright, 1935, by Noel Coward. Reprinted by permission of Doubleday, Doran & Co., Inc.

about fifty yards of the main river and collapsed—I'd
been going for twelve days. I was torn to bits by thorns,
and the blood-poisoning had given me a fever. Then suddenly I heard the hooter of a steamer, quite close, and I
staggered up and started yelling like mad; then about a
quarter of an hour later I heard it again—in the distance.
Then I knew I was done for because steamers only go
down that river once or twice a month at most. So I just
lay down on the ground. . . . Then halfway through the
next day I sort of came to my senses for a bit, and struggled on to the actual bank of the river, and just by a fluke
there happened to be a solitary Indian passing in a canoe.
If I'd been five minutes later he wouldn't have seen me.
But he did, thank God, and he got me down river to San
José, where an old Brazilian priest looked after me until
I was well enough to be moved to São Paolo. . . . It was
pretty awful.

NOAH [1]

by

ANDRE OBEY

English text by Arthur Wilmurt

NOAH *has just finished building the ark. It is in the middle of a forest. He is a kindly man, adored by his family,
but suspected by the villagers of causing the three months
of drought. He is very serious.*

NOAH *is taking measurements of the ark and singing a
little song. He scratches his head and goes over the measurements again. Then he calls.*

NOAH. (*Softly.*) Lord . . . (*Louder.*) Lord . . . (*Very
loud.*) Lord! . . . Yes, Lord, it's me. Terribly sorry to

[1] Copyright, 1934, by A. Wilmurt.

bother You again, but . . . What? Yes, I know You've
other things to think of, but after I've shoved off, won't
it be a little late? . . . Oh, no, Lord, no, no, no. . . . Now,
Lord, please don't think that. . . . Oh, but look, of course
I trust You! You could tell me to set sail on a plank—on a
branch—on just a cabbage leaf. . . . Why, You could tell
me to put out to sea with nothing but my loincloth, even
without my loincloth—completely— (*He has gone down
on his knees, but he gets up immediately.*) Yes, yes, I beg
Your pardon. Your time is precious. Well, this is all I
wanted to ask: Should I make a rudder? I say, a rudder.
. . . No, no. R as in Robert; U as in Hubert; D as in . . .
that's it, a rudder. Ah, good . . . very good, very good.
The winds, the current, the tides. . . . What was that,
Lord? The tempests? Oh, and while I have You, one other
little question. . . . Are you listening, Lord? (*To the
audience.*) Gone!! . . . He's in a temper. . . . Well, you
can't blame Him; He has so much to think of. All right;
no rudder. (*He considers the ark.*) The tides, the currents,
the winds. (*He imitates the winds.*) Psch! . . . Psch! . . .
The tempests. (*He imitates the tempests.*) Vloum! Ba da
Bloum! . . . That's going to be something. (*He makes a
quick movement.*)—magnificent!! . . . No, no, Lord, I'm
not afraid. I know that You'll be with me. I was just trying
to imagine . . . Oh, Lord, while You're there I'd like to
ask . . . (*To audience.*) Chc! Gone again. You see how
careful you have to be. (*He laughs.*) He was listening all
the time. (*He goes to the ark.*) Tempests. . . . I'm going
to put a few more nails in down here. (*He hammers and
sings.*)

> When the boat goes well, all goes well.
> When all goes well, the boat goes well.

(*He admires his work.*) And when I think that a year
ago I couldn't hammer a tack without mashing a nail.
That's pretty good, if I do say so myself. (*He climbs aboard
the ark and stands there like a captain.*) Larboard and
starboard! . . . Cast off! . . . Close the portholes! . . .

'Ware shoals! . . . Wait till the squall's over. . . . Good!
. . . Fine! . . . Now I'm ready, completely ready, super-
ready! (*He cries to Heaven.*) I am ready! (*Then quietly.*)
There, I'd like to know how this business is going to begin. (*He looks all around, at the trees, the bushes, and
the sky.*) The weather is magnificent, the heat—oppressive,
and there's not a sign of a cloud. Well, that part of the
program is His affair.

CANDLELIGHT [1]

by

Siegfried Geyer

Adapted by P. G. Wodehouse

JOSEF, *valet to* PRINCE RUDOLF, *is a charming and attractive young man. The* PRINCE *is called away unexpectedly
and asks* JOSEF *to cancel an engagement for him.*

JOSEF *returns; closes door center. He takes a cigarette
from box, lights it and smokes luxuriantly. Draws the
memorandum pad from his pocket, searching for* LISERL'S
*address, humming, and reclines on sofa with head toward
center.*

JOSEF.   Laura—Lina—Lola—Lehman's   Steam   Laundry
—Liserl—Seventy-eight-Three-Ninety-five. (*Reaches for
phone.*) Seventy-eight-Three-Ninety-five, please— Pardon?
Seventy-eight— What? I was ringing Central. Ring off,
please. (*Puts phone back in box; takes up phone again.*)
Seventy-eight-Three-Ninety-five, please. Hullo, is this Central? Well, but that's the— What number?—What?—Ring
off, please. (*Again puts phone back in box, then once
more takes up phone.*) Hullo? Is this Central? No? What
is it? *You* again? For goodness' sake— Can't you— (*His

*manner suddenly changes. He has just realized that it is
an attractive voice which is speaking—coos.*) What a sweet
voice you have! (*He listens and smiles.*) Me? Oh, *my*
voice isn't sweet. No, really? My dear lady, you make me
blush. (*With sudden indignation.*) A tenor? I'm not a
tenor, I'm a light baritone. (*Sweetly once more.*) No, of
course I'm not offended. Even tenors are God's creatures,
aren't they? Ha! Ha! What a delightful laugh you have—
Do go on. Yes, go on laughing. I could listen to you laughing forever. . . . What sort of a man am I? Well, why
don't you come around and see?—Oh, do. Pop into your
car and come round. I'm a most respectable person. Oh,
yes, just a gentleman of leisure. One of the idle rich, you
know. Do come and cheer my loneliness. What lovely teeth
you have— Eh? Oh, yes, you can always tell by a woman's
voice—what sort of teeth she has. I don't know. It's something in the way she pronounces the word "No." But why
say *no?* Oh, don't ring off. Please don't ring off. Those
whom Central has joined together let no man put asunder.
You can't come? Why not? Your husband out? He must
be or you wouldn't be able to stay at the phone so long.
You're not sure you want to? But it is your duty. What
nobler mission can a woman have than to cheer a lonely
man? You *will* come?—Wonderful! Eleven Ringstrasse
is the address. Apartment number three on the first floor.
Oh, yes, a very exclusive neighborhood. Yes, goodbye.
(JOSEF *puts phone back in box and starts right joyfully.*)

THE BISHOP MISBEHAVES [1]

by

FREDERICK JACKSON

The BISHOP OF BROADMINSTER *and his sister stop at a pub
to telephone home to say that they have been delayed*

[1] Copyright, 1935, by Frederick Jackson.

by the storm. The BISHOP *is an elderly gentleman, kindly, humorous and extremely curious.*

BISHOP. (*Stops just outside the door and looks about—surprised at finding the place deserted. Calling out loudly.*) Shop!—I say, is anyone about?—Shop!—I want to telephone. (*He looks about, going left a little.*) Odd! Very odd! (*He looks right and sees the bottle of champagne on the table. Goes across to it. Picks up the bottle and reads the label.*) LeRoy! (*Puts the bottle back on table.* LADY EMILY LYONS, *the* BISHOP's *sister, comes in from left center. . . .*) My dear Emily. I asked you to wait in the car. This is not quite the place for you. . . . It must be respectable. There's a picture of Queen Victoria. . . . Unfortunately, however, one cannot always trust to appearances. It seems to me too quiet and respectable to ring quite true. (*Looking at his watch.*) Not yet closing time. One would expect the proprietor to be on hand. Of course there was that big motor car abandoned at the door. There may be private rooms and the proprietor may be detained there. . . . (*Going toward the bar.*) Naturally! [I would prefer to have stepped into some gruesome mystery.]— Wouldn't you? . . . I don't hope that a crime has happened here. I only hope that if a crime has happened—it has happened here. You see the distinction, my dear? . . . (*At left center.*) This little adventure begins, you may observe, as so many detective stories do begin. Strangers coming into an old inn at night—and finding no one about—the place deserted and uncannily quiet—and I've always wanted to be personally involved in a mystery. . . . But one can't read too many detective stories, my dear Emily. And I like them to influence the way I think. I mean, they stimulate the imagination—they exercise one's mental faculties— they make one observant. Of course, there are good ones and bad ones. But I attribute my quick, ingenious brain entirely to my almost exclusive diet of detective fiction. I only regret that my duties to the church prevent my plac-

ing my gifts at the service of humanity. In fact, I sometimes feel I might have done greater good if I had been a
Scotland Yard man. (*He takes a silver snuff box from his
pocket, sniffs a pinch of snuff and sneezes.*) I mean it, my
dear. (*He goes up to the fire, "snooping" about the mantel.*)
After all, my parishioners are never really wicked. Alas,
no, their sins are only petty sins. Hardly worthy of my
attention. Now, one who has a natural talent along these
lines, developed to a certain extent by reading— (*He picks
up* WALLER's *hat from the chair and looks inside it.*) might
be wasted in the church. You know I can always solve the
problem before I have read five chapters. (*He goes toward
the bar.*) . . . It is really most odd that no one comes.
There were people here just before we arrived. . . . (*Mys-
teriously.*) Clues! . . . Circumstantial evidence, my dear.
(*Pointing to ash tray on table left.*) Fresh cigarettes—
(*Pointing to table right.*) That unopened bottle of champagne— (*Pointing to* WALLER's *hat.*) A gentleman's hat—
(*Looking about the floor up left center.*) Foot-prints.
(*Goes to the bar and picks up glass left there by* HESTER.)
And those glasses, still on the bar. (*Sniffs the glass.*) Gin
and tonic. A woman drank from that glass. . . . Lipstick.
(*Puts the glass down. Picks up whiskey glass left by* RED
and sniffs it.) Whiskey! (*Looking at the glass closely.*)
No lipstick! (*Takes a small magnifying glass from his
pocket and studies the glass.*) A man! Big, coarse, brutal
fellow too. (*Takes a pinch of snuff from the box, sprinkles
it on the glass, blows it off and studies the glass.*) Fingerprint.—Thumb! (*The* BISHOP *stands meditating.* . . .) I
was just wondering. They didn't leave by the front door
or we'd have seen them. And if they left sometime before
we arrived, why are the glasses still on the bar?—Bar-
tenders always remove the glasses immediately—I've noticed
that. Why didn't this one?—Interrupted, no doubt, by the
arrival of the party in the big car at the door. But where
is the party and— (*Loudly.*) Where is the barman?—
Shop!—I say! (EMILY *goes to the door at right.* . . . *She*

knocks timidly on the door then listens. His attention caught.) What is it, my dear? (*Goes to her.*) . . . Scuffling? . . . (*She opens the door cautiously and peers in, closes the door quickly with little gasp and jumps back against the* BISHOP.) . . . (*In a whisper.*) Is it the body? . . . [Three people. Bound and gagged.] Ah! Then it's not a murder. Only a stick-up. One moment, my dear, I'll release them. (*Goes into the room.*)

A MURDER HAS BEEN ARRANGED [1]

by

EMLYN WILLIAMS

SIR CHARLES *is about to celebrate his fortieth birthday with a party on the stage of a theatre. He is to inherit two million pounds if he is still alive at eleven o'clock.* MAURICE MULLINS, *who is the next heir, has planned to murder* SIR CHARLES. *He is young, attractive and well poised. He is talking to* SIR CHARLES' *secretary who knows him for what he is.*

MULLINS. (*He rises and surveys the theatre coolly.*) There's something about a theatre that always makes me want to make a speech. (*He advances to the footlights and looks out into the darkness of the auditorium.*) . . . I've studied myself for years, and I've always been interested in my subject. Here are my conclusions. Some men are born good. They grow up to be saints, or heroes, or preachers, or ideal husbands, as the case may be. Maurice Austin Mullins, however, was born bad. Very bad indeed. I like to be very well dressed, to feel very comfortable in a very big car, with the knowledge that if it breaks down, I have seven others just as big to choose from. I like to buy for every woman I like, everything she likes. I like caviare, champagne. Not because I enjoy the stuff, but because it's so . . . so gloriously, expensive. Anybody can forge a check. . . . That's where my artist touch comes in. The good men have their code of sport; I have mine. . . . The little nobodies forge their checks with a trembling hand and a sidelong eye, in the quiet of their bedrooms; I forge mine in public, with a flourish, as if I were signing a letter bequeathing a thousand pounds to the Girls' Friendly Society. I've been fulfilling my destiny ever since I extracted chocolates from slot machines with incredible ingenuity. I've been borrowing money, stealing money . . . ever since I can remember. I don't take furtive sniffs at the cup of vice. I drink it to the dregs, with a gesture. I am the Complete Criminal. . . . Think of the stake! Two million pounds.—Think of the danger! That attracts me enormously. In my time I've dabbled a dirty finger in nearly every pie, but never this! . . . The danger! The incredible danger! They'll turn that will on me like a great devastating searchlight. The probability of my having done it will be so enormous they'll *know* I did it, but I'll do it in such a way they can never prove it! You watch me win—

FOR ONE WOMAN

DODSWORTH [1]

by

SINCLAIR LEWIS

Dramatized by Sidney Howard

FRAN DODSWORTH *is a selfish, restless woman. To satisfy her, her husband has sold the business to which he has devoted his life so that he may take her on an extended trip to Europe.*

FRAN. I suppose you feel kind of lost. . . . You mustn't feel lost, though. I mean, that will wear off. Life isn't going to be empty from now on. It's going to be fuller than ever! And richer! For both of us, Sam! Think! You're free! After twenty years of doing what was expected of us, *we're* free! Don't look so mournful about it, darling! Is that the wrong thing for me to say? I'm sorry! It all seems so exciting to me! . . . Oh, but I want much more than a trip out of this, Sam! I want a new life all over from the beginning! A perfectly glorious, free, adventurous life! And it's coming to both of us, Sam! Haven't we earned it? . . . Why, I'd . . . I'd almost sell this house, so we wouldn't have anything to tie us down! . . . What I want is to get us some new selves now! . . . Give yourself a chance to enjoy your leisure and you'll see! Why, you might get to be an ambassador, Sam! . . . Yes, you might, easily! Why, if we weren't tied to this deadly, half-baked Middle-Western town! . . . I'm not knocking Zenith, Sam!

... (*Vehemently.*) I'm thinking of my freedom, too! And I want the lovely things I've got a right to! In Europe a woman of my age is just getting to where men take a serious interest in her! And I just won't be put on the shelf by my daughter when I can still dance better and longer than she can! I've got brains and, thank God, I've still got looks! And no one ever takes me for more than thirty-five—or thirty, even! I'm begging for life, Sam! No, I'm not! I'm demanding it!

DAISY MAYME [1]

by

George Kelly

DAISY MAYME PLUNKETT *is a hearty, frank woman with a keen sense of humor. While on a holiday, she meets* CLIFF *and his niece. She comes to visit them and finds* CLIFF *ensnared by his relatives.*

MISS PLUNKETT. (MISS PLUNKETT *rests her elbow on the keyboard and turns to* CLIFF.) You know it's a funny thing, though, Cliff,—people think you're crazy any more if you laugh. (*He is amused.*) That's a positive fact. I catch people looking at me all the time as though I didn't have a grain of sense. I know your sister Laura here thinks I'm completely gone. . . . And Olly thinks I never *was* here. . . . But, I should worry. (*She strikes a rather ambitious chord on the piano.*) Any time I can't laugh, I want to call it a day. (*Turning to* CLIFF.) What else is there to it, Cliff, if you don't get a laugh? . . . There's nothing at all that I can see. Going around with one of those faces that looks as though it got caught in a wringer. (. . . MISS PLUNKETT *turns to the piano again.*) Not me. Give me liberty or give

[1] Copyright, 1926, 1927, by George Kelly. Reprinted by permission of Little, Brown & Co., Boston.

me laughs. And you can have the liberty. (*She strikes a few more notes. . . . Then she drops her hands into her lap and looks rather wistfully at the keyboard.*) I wish I could play the piano. . . . That was the dream of my life when I was a kid, to take music lessons. . . . We couldn't afford it. I didn't have the time, anyway; I was kept too busy doing housework and minding the other kids. But I was always pretending I could play, on the table; we didn't have a piano. . . . You don't play, do you Cliff? . . . Anything. Any games or anything. . . . (*Rising slowly and coming towards him.*) You ought to make a little time, Cliff. There's something else in life besides slaving all your days. And what are you slaving for? To leave it to a lot of relatives to fight over. . . . I think it's a terrible thing to let yourself be cheated out of life. Of course, it's all right to do the right thing by people, but be sure you do the right thing by yourself while you're at it. Because half the time they don't appreciate it. And then where do you get off? Just a funny old bird that never married. Good picking for them, if you happen to have a few dollars. I've been through it all, Cliff; nobody can tell me anything about it. It was a great joke at home whenever a fellow looked at me. They used to laugh me out of it. One of those eldest daughter things. I wasn't supposed to marry; I was needed at home, to wait on the rest of them. But the minute they took a notion to go,—try and stop them. The last of them went about four years ago; and left me nice and flat, out in the alley—at thirty-five years of age—without a home or a job. A couple of them offered me a home, but because I wouldn't let their kids kick me in the shins and say nothing, I was just a cranky old maid. And their mothers thought it was funny. So I dropped them all cold after a bit and started a little store. Dry goods and notions—mostly notions. I didn't know how to do anything else—but housework. But it turned out all right, thank God! I have a nice little business now; and my own dollar. And that's the way I'm going to stay, too.

And they've all been eating out of my hand ever since. And believe me, they don't eat anything out of my hand unless they earn it, either. So much for so much. Any time any of them want anything out of me, they come right down to my store and work for it. And it's been the making of a couple of them. (*She folds her arms and rocks back and forth narrowing her eyes shrewdly. . . .*) I think I'll play the piano some more. (*She moves up the middle of the room towards the piano.*) . . . Sometimes. [I'm sorry I didn't marry.] (*She leans against the piano and looks thoughtfully at the floor.*) Although if I had I wouldn't know as much as I know now. Of course I might have been happier, but I think it's better to be wise than happy: because if you're wise you've always got something; and if you're just happy,—you haven't. (*She sits down at the piano.*) Besides, I think if you're going to marry, you should do it when you're young;—go through the hard days together; then there'll be something to keep you together when the good ones come.

NINE TILL SIX [1]

by

AIMÉE AND PHILIP STUART

MRS. PEMBROKE *is a serene, middle-aged woman who owns a very fashionable Millinery and Dressmaking Shop in London. She has had to struggle all her life with the shop in order to support her three children. An apprentice has been caught stealing a dress. The stock-keeper defends the girl, saying the help aren't paid enough.*

MRS. PEMBROKE. . . . Now then, Freda, let me have my say. You ask us to look at what we make. Do you think that's a great deal? . . . Now let's take the whole year. We have

[1] Copyright, 1930, by Aimée and Philip Stuart. Reprinted by permission of the authors.

four driving months; six when we just manage to jog along, and two when we're so slack that we think the world's come to an end. In the meantime the expenses go on. Do you know the rent of this shop? . . . We pay by the inch. The workrooms are extra. For the shop alone we pay a yearly rental of seven thousand five hundred pounds—with rates and taxes, ten thousand pounds. . . . We're in one of the best streets. . . . Were you with me when I took that little place upstairs? . . . I paid a third of the rent and had what's known as a "Select Clientele!" Give me "Customers!" What you don't seem to realize, Freda, is that what we sell isn't all profit. . . . Now, take your department alone! You know the cost price of materials nowadays, don't you? . . . But what you don't know is that I only just manage to make both ends meet. With all my responsibility, I make very little more out of it than you do. I sometimes wonder if it's worth while going on. The strain is too great. It takes us all our time to keep pace. Since the War we shopkeepers have had too much to fight against. Everything hits back—weather, strikes, political situations, Royal illnesses, cost of production, cost of a roof over our heads, and it gets worse and worse. (*With a complete change of tone.*) I've an old-fashioned horror of bankruptcy. I'd rather get out while I can pay what I owe. If I do, I shall be on the market with you, Freda. But you'll stand more chance. You're younger than I am. . . . You're quite right—wages are not high enough—nothing like high enough! But they're too high for those that have to find them at the end of the week. The fault lies with conditions that cripple employed and employer alike. How those conditions are to be coped with I don't know—but I do know that they're killing individual enterprise—and here speaks an old horse that's been tied to the cart all its life! . . . You're quite right to feel resentment against conditions that make the day's work seem a drudgery. I feel resentment against conditions that make me seem a tyrant. But we're both helpless. At least let us be friends.

MARY OF SCOTLAND [1]

by

MAXWELL ANDERSON

The scene is a prison room. After years of scheming QUEEN ELIZABETH *holds* MARY *her prisoner offering her freedom if she will abdicate her crown.*

MARY. Stay now a moment. I begin to glimpse
Behind this basilisk mask of yours. It was this
You've wanted from the first. . . .
It was you sent Lord Throgmorton long ago
When first I'd have married Bothwell. All this while
Some evil's touched my life at every turn.
To cripple what I'd do. And now—why now—
Looking on you—I see it incarnate before me—
It was your hand that touched me. Reaching out
In little ways—here a word, there an action—this
Was what you wanted. I thought perhaps a star—
Wildly I thought it—perhaps a star might ride
Astray—or a crone that burned an image down
In wax—filling the air with curses on me
And slander; the murder of Rizzio, Moray in that
And you behind Moray—the murder of Darnley, Throg-
    morton
Behind that too, you with them—and that winged scandal
You threw at us when we were married. Proof I have none
But I've felt it—would know it anywhere—in your eyes—
There—before me. . . .
I see how I came.
Back, back, each step the wrong way, and each sign followed
As you'd have me go, till the skein picks up and we stand
Face to face here. It was you forced Bothwell from me—

You there, and always. Oh, I'm to blame in this, too!
I should have seen your hand! . . .
And suppose indeed you won
Within our life-time, still looking down from the heavens
And up from men around us, God's spies that watch
The fall of great and little, they will find you out—
I will wait for that, wait longer than a life,
Till men and the times unscroll you, study the tricks
You play, and laugh, as I shall laugh, being known
Your better, haunted by your demon, driven
To death or exile by you, unjustly. Why,
When all's done, it's my name I care for, my name and
    heart,
To keep them clean. Win now, take your triumph now,
For I'll win men's hearts in the end—though the sifting
    takes
This hundred years—or a thousand.

ACCENT ON YOUTH [1]

by

Samson Raphaelson

LINDA *has come to see* STEVEN GAYE, *a playwright, for whom
she worked as secretary and later played a lead in his play.
He is considerably older than she. She was very much in
love with him until she met* DICKIE, *a boy of her own age
whom she married.*

LINDA. You've got to take me back. You don't know what
I've been through. I've been in hell for five months. No
matter what I've done to you, I've paid for it. I lead a life
of torture—it's become a nightmare—you're the only one
who can save me. . . . I thought I did. [Love him when I

married him.] It all happened so quickly, how could I tell? I married him that same night—I left the show—you were so mean about everything, I hated you . . . I could have loved him; I wanted to; I tried.—And then came the honeymoon . . . I never want to go through anything like it again. Oh, Steven, why didn't you tell me what a dreadful thing youth was—why didn't anybody tell me!—We went to Santa Barbara. Here's a typical honeymoon day: out of bed at seven—A.M. not P.M.—three hasty kisses, a shower, then we play tennis—what do I know about tennis? Then, sweating and limp, another shower, two hasty kisses, and swimming, while I sit on the beach and burn.—Did you ever see the rich men's sons in their bathing suits waiting for the depression to pass? They're broad-shouldered, handsome, tan—every one of them was once an All-American something—and ten feet away you can't tell one from the other . . . and you couldn't tell Dickie from any of them.—Then he gets a rub-down and it's time for lunch. Oh, Steven, after sitting with a clean-cut outdoors man and watching him eat vitamins, starches and spinach, you and your pills are a Midsummer Night's Dream.—Going to bed with him was just like going to bed with the front page of a physical culture magazine: in the first place, I was too exhausted by that time to care for him even if I hadn't begun to hate him; and there you lie, unable to sleep because the lights are on—and why are the lights on? Because Lionel Strongfort has to do his setting-up exercises: it seems that somewhere during the day he missed out on a couple of muscles.—Then a home in Connecticut, fox-hunting, golf, polo. . . . Five months of it, Steven—five months without night life, without the theatre, without glasses of beer pounding the table because somebody has got something crazy and beautiful and passionate to say to somebody else, without cigarettes and poetry and laughter and bad ventilation, without dialogue—without you, Steven. . . .

LOVER'S LEAP [1]

by

PHILIP JOHNSON

HELEN STORER *is an attractive woman of thirty-five. She has lived very happily and comfortably in her country house since her husband left her seven years ago. In spite of her own experience she is trying to justify marriage to her sister and her sister's fiancé.*

HELEN. (*Rising.*) Don't you see . . . our experience was—well, there were exceptional circumstances. . . . You see, it was all a matter of—well—I suppose you'd call it temperament. His and mine. . . . They were opposed, utterly opposed. . . . it was a tragedy. . . . We loved one another and yet, somehow, we couldn't help getting on one another's nerves. We hated making one another miserable; but that didn't prevent us from doing it. . . . (*To* SARAH.) [We quarrelled.] But never about anything that really mattered. (*To* CEDRIC.) It was all so silly! Childish! (*She moves to table and takes cigarette.*) There's no denying, of course, that Roger *was* difficult. . . . I'm trying to look at it all quite dispassionately, so that I may help you. . . . We'll say he had some irritating qualities. (*A pause while she lights her cigarette.*) While I, of course, had my share. . . . I was very silly, I'm afraid, about lots of things. . . . Thunderstorms, for instance. (*Sighing.*) It's stupid of me, but the first rumble of thunder sends me scuttling off in a panic to the boot-cupboard. . . . I keep a bottle of sherry and a tin of Marie biscuits there now, on purpose. . . . My husband, though, could never understand my being scared, and he'd be all freezingly calm and just pour out statistics and things to prove I'd no right to be afraid.

And the more he talked, the worse I'd get, until the whole thing would explode in a violent scene. (*Reminiscently.*) It was during one of our thunderstorm quarrels, I remember, that I bit his finger. . . . Right through to the bone. . . . And then there was his Egyptology. (*About to sit.*) . . . Every hour he spent poring over those drab books, or wandering round some dreary museum, I regarded as a deliberate insult to myself. (*Sits.*) . . . And in the end Egypt won. (*She sighs.*) He just walked out of the house one night, saying that he was going to take the dog for a walk. He left a note on the hall-table, and the next I heard from him was a postcard from Gibraltar.

MR. FAITHFUL [1]

by

Lord Dunsany

MRS. JAM, *a child's nurse, is about fifty. She does not know that* DICK, *of whom she complains, has a job as watchdog to* SIR WALTER WAMPLE *to whom she speaks.* DICK *has acquired the habits of a dog and acts like one.*

MRS. JAM. [I've come.] About a young gentleman, Sir, what I learns lives here. Goes along the Serpentine, he does—near the edge where the ducks are—you was walking along some way in front; I recognizes your face; walking along quite nice and respectable, you was; not a word to say against it; but he was a-dancing and a-romping, and I goes there naturally like we all does, with my little boy in his pram, Lady Cheedle's little boy, a little dear, and his handful of bread and all, and there is this young gentleman romping along the edge of the water, which I takes no notice of him at first, being intent on feeding the ducks, which little Master Tom 'ad set 'is heart on. So 'e sees a duck in the water—quack-quack he always calls them because of the noise they make—and "Quack-quack," he says, "Come 'ere." The duck looks up, seeming to understand like, and little Master Tom 'e throws his bread. And at that this here young gentleman he ups and comes romping along, and he gets hold of Master Tom's bread, and he *eats* it if you please; which, saving your presence, was a wicked act, and broke Master Tom's heart. . . . It isn't 'im as wants the bread, which he'd have a whole bakery given him every day if he wanted it, it's 'is poor quack-quack as he calls it. Doesn't seem to rest proper at night thinking of the poor duck out in the cold without its bread, and a great large gentleman like that eating it, which I'm ashamed of him. . . . It's a wicked thing, Sir, a large gentleman like him and I won't rest till something's done about it; and, as for my bus-fare here, it's already been paid by a nice kind gentleman what saw it all happen and told me where you lived and one thing and another. . . . (*Recognizing* DICK.) It's 'im, Sir! It's 'im what was robbing innocent ducks on their nest, of their hard-earned bread and all. I wonder 'e had the face to look at me after his wickedness, him with his romping ways and his feet in the water, behaving more like an I-don't-know-what in the zoo than like a human being. . . . (*Somewhat mollified.*) Well, if you take steps, Sir, well and good; and if you hadn't, it would have had to be the police; which it's not that I'm vindictive, but sheer wickedness I won't stand. . . . Well, then I'll be going back to Chester Square, where such doings is never thought of. (*With one contemptuous glance at* DICK.) Seem to think yourself a camel-leopard. (*Exit right.*)

NO MORE LADIES [1]

by

A. E. THOMAS

FANNY TOWNSEND *is a very brisk, independent old lady, who enjoys life thoroughly. She is the pet of her family, and knows it. She is talking to a young man, and surprising him considerably, which means that she is having a fine time.*

FANNY. It's a woman's business to look attractive. She must interest the beholder—by hook or by crook—or else she's sunk. . . . There's art in it, young man. . . . Yes—art. I don't know many old ladies. I don't cultivate 'em—don't like 'em—much. But I see a lot of 'em as I go around this town, and most of 'em give me a swift pain. Bobbed hair—well, that's all right—neat, anyhow—but beauty parlors, rouge and calcimine and the airs and graces of youth—to me they are asinine. . . . Well, I saw all these things coming along—all my contemporaries growing to look more and more like a lot of superannuated ballet dancers. And I saw I had to make up my mind about it and I did. Even when skirts were short, mine never were. . . . I suppose really, it was my legs. . . . I never liked 'em much. But that's not all. The fact is, when I go out, as I do a great deal people notice me. I look like something out of the Mauve Decade. People smile and nudge each other and I can hear them whisper. "Oh, look—isn't she quaint" —. . . The fact is I stand out. And I admit I like it. . . . I do. [Enjoy life.] It's a great show and I've got an aisle seat in the front row, maybe it wouldn't be so nice if I had to sit in the top gallery. . . . I mean I'm independent. I've my own apartment, my own maid, my own car and chauffeur. And I do as I damn well please. I go out when I like and come home when I'm ready. I shall go to Palm

Beach in February, and to Paris in June; and the fact that
I've quite a bit of money that unfortunately I can't be able
to take with me when I shuffle off, confers on me a pleasant,
if slightly spurious popularity with my friends and relatives. . . . But if I'm a dependent, I have to take orders
disguised of course, as suggestion. Oh yes, but a rotten egg,
my dear young man, is a rotten egg, no matter how you
cook it.

OUTWARD BOUND [1]

by

Sutton Vane

*The scene is a ship's lounge. The passengers do not realize
that they are dead, and that they are outward bound to
meet the great examiner.* MRS. CLIVEDEN-BANKS *is "a withered
old harridan of fifty-odd—probably once beautiful."*

MRS. CLIVEDEN-BANKS. I saw your name on the passenger
list, so I asked for the bar at once, and here you are! (*Sits
left of table.*) . . . [I am] Joining my dear husband. And
I'm afraid we're in for a very dull trip. There is nobody
on board—at least nobody who *is* anybody. Though, of
course, the poor creatures can't help that. You follow me.
What I say I mean in the most kindly manner—but still,
there it is. . . . By the way, my name is *Cliveden*-Banks.
You know, of course, but it's such a long while since we
met. There was a plain Mrs. Banks in the divorce court
lately—so silly of her—and so plain, judging from the
Daily Mirror—a total stranger, of course. Still it's made me
very particular about my hyphen. Not that I am ever likely
to appear in a divorce court. . . . When I said there was
nobody on board, dear Mr. Prior, between you and me,
there is one person on board to whom I shall take a strong

objection. He's a clergyman. . . . Clergymen at sea are dreadfully unlucky. We shall probably all go to the bottom. If we do I shall blame the clergyman entirely. In my opinion steamship companies have no right to let clergymen travel at all. The clergy ought to stay at home in their own parishes and do good, not go gadding about all over the world putting other people's lives in danger. . . . Well, the best thing we can do is to cut the fellow dead. Nicely, of course, but firmly. . . . (*The* REV. WILLIAM DUKE *enters.*) . . . Benjamin, I regret to say, is feeling the heat dreadfully. I should have joined him last year, but somehow I never got time. The penalty of popularity. My great friend, Mabel, the Duchess of Middleford—*you don't* know her, of course, she was only saying to me at the Palace the other day—. . . Who is that man? . . . How strange! Peculiar people one must meet, mustn't one, in public places? Never mind. Let me see, where was I? . . . Oh, yes, of course. And then that strange man whom we neither of us know interrupted by wishing you good morning. Never mind. Mabel pointed out to me very clearly that I was in danger of neglecting my duty. She said to me quite plainly, almost brutally, and she can be very brutal sometimes—"My dear Genevieve," she said, "you must remember you are a daughter of the Empire, a soldier's *daughter*—a soldier's *wife*. Your place is by your husband's side in far, far India." In fact she was so insistent on my leaving England that if I didn't know her really well, I should have felt she wanted to get rid of me. Still I have taken her advice, I have abandoned London's gaieties and go to help poor dear Benjamin rule a lot of black men. Frankly I hate the idea.

BRIEF CANDLE [1]

by

RObert HAre PowEL

CYNTHIA, *a romantic young woman, leaves a gay, Newport party. She wanders into a beautiful, moonlit garden where she meets the owner, an attractive young man. She tells him why she likes the garden.*

CYNTHIA. . . . You see, long ago and once upon a time—there was a small, awkward girl with a vivid imagination and romantic ideas. . . . Do you really want me to go on? . . . Well, one of her dreams was a garden where there was everything she wanted. It was full of roses and surrounded by a high wall. . . . Like this. It kept the world away. The only people who could ever get into it were her own make-believe ones. They understood her perfectly and never called her silly or anything like that. She used to spend a lot of her time there. It was very easy. All she had to do was to shut her eyes. . . . (CYNTHIA *shuts hers.*) One day her family took her to France and left her in a convent and it was there she found her garden. . . . She'd dream in it and watch her phantom people pass. One of them was a shining Knight who fought under her colors. She'd bind up his wounds and then he'd drink her health by moonlight in champagne and call her "Fair Lady"! (*Laughs. Opens her eyes.*) . . . One day she left her garden and never went back. In fact she'd almost forgotten it till she stepped in here to-night—Journey's End! . . . That's all.

[1] Copyright, 1929, by Robert Hare Powel; revised, 1934, by Robert Hare Powel.

THE NOOSE [1]

by

WILLARD MACK

From a story by H. H. VAN LOAN

DOT DAWLY *is a night club entertainer. She is quite young, and very sweet and sincere. She has been not in the least hardened or influenced by any of the shady characters with whom she has come in contact. The scene is the Governor's mansion.*

DOT. I want to see the Governor—. . . (*Pauses as she looks at him.*) *Sure.* (*She remembers here she has seen his picture.*) . . . (*Hurriedly.*) I was over to the jail, and they wouldn't let me in—without a pass—so I came over here, the man that brought me in said—. . . It's kinda hard for me to get started, 'cause you see—I ain't never talked to a big man like you before—I—. . . Nickie—that's it—it's about Nickie. (*She falters, the tears come.*) I am Dot Dawly—I worked in the club where he hung out— I was there the night he croaked Gordon. (*Turning away to front.*) . . . I didn't have no idea of coming until last night—but, after the show we all sat around just waiting for *the hour* to come—and—Dave Stern and Big Jack and some of the rest of us got talking about Nickie— you see it's been awful lonesome without him—around the club—and nobody could help him at the trial 'cause he wouldn't say nothing—so we just sat there thinking that it was only five hours till you bumped him off over here. (*She stops and bursts out crying.*) . . . So there we sat and waited and then some one, it was my pal Patsy I think, she got to thinking what was going to happen to Nickie when it was all over— (*Cries very softly.*) . . . So we took up a collection, everybody chipped in—even the musicians. . . . An' it amounted to near three hundred bucks, an' that's enough to send him off right—ain't it sir? (*Moving a step or two nearer him.*) You see—he ain't got no relatives, ain't even got a father and mother, he told me—so nobody wants it but us—. . . Nickie—his body—. . . (*Moving to front of chair, between it and desk. This speech is spoken with heart-broken and hysterical and pathetic emotion and tears with absolutely no heroics.*) That's what I came over for—ain't no reason why I can't have it—is there—if nobody else wants it—? (*She sinks her head on the desk, handkerchief clasped in her hand sobbing softly but convulsively. Pause, her handkerchief is in her right hand which she has been using occasionally through the scene.*) . . . (*Scarcely crediting what she has heard, raising up but leaves handkerchief on desk.*) They didn't—hang him—? . . . He ain't dead—he's going to get a—what do you call it? . . . (*Backing away just to clear the chair.*) If it's all the same to you, sir, I won't come [back this afternoon] and please, don't never tell him I was here. . . . (*Comes towards desk right of it.*) I was always crazy about him—even if he never gave me a tumble. But—there's a girl—somewhere—'cause Nickie told me he wanted to have a wife—and a home—and go straight. He told me that the night he shot Gordon. And he talked about her. (*Backing away slowly towards door a few steps.*) And, if he lives, I'll find out who she is—and fix it up between them. So you see—there's no use telling Nickie—about me. . . . You see—caring about him—that was the reason *I came.* He never gave me a break while he was out and around so I thought that when he was dead I could take the body away somewhere to a little cemetery I know, and then I could go there once in a while and tell him the things I couldn't say when he was alive—see? (*Backing away to door until she is against it, until her right hand is on the knob of it. She breaks again.*) But there ain't no need—now. I'll tell the folks—at the club—what a regular you've been—to me. We didn't know you were— (*Stops. Starts to exit.*) . . . (*Turns. Eagerly.*) See Nickie? . . . Oh—could I? . . . Gee—you're a square shooter. (*Exits.*)

FOR ONE MAN AND ONE WOMAN

MRS. MOONLIGHT [1]

by

BENN W. LEVY

TOM MOONLIGHT *is a man about forty. He is very much in love with his wife,* SARAH, *and she with him.* SARAH *has a necklace around which has grown a legend that every owner may have a wish come true. She wished to keep her youth and beauty.*

TOM. Old married people, indeed! (*She is at the mirror.*) Look at the old married lady in front of you!

SARAH. (*Seriously, with a glance that is almost haunted.*) I look my years.

TOM. You don't. (*She closes her eyes at a sudden stab of pain. What a strange girl it is!*) And for that matter, if I may say so, I don't keep too badly myself in a dry place. Look your years! It's my belief you never will.

SARAH. (*A little wildly.*) Please, Tom! You know that hurts —that hateful subject.

TOM. I'm sorry, dear. I thought you were over that silly fancy.

SARAH. Tom.

TOM. Yes, dear.

SARAH. I'm frightened.

TOM. Frightened? What of?

SARAH. Come and sit by me. (*He sits by her, holding her hand. She is definitely trembling.*) Supposing, Tom, supposing someone should be born who never really did grow any older; I mean, after a certain age. At least, who never looked any older. What would happen?

41

TOM. She'd probably make a fortune in a freak show.

SARAH. Please be serious, Tom.

TOM. How can I be serious about such nonsense?

SARAH. But just supposing. What do you think would happen?

TOM. Well, in the olden times she'd probably have been burnt as a witch.

SARAH. And what nowadays?

TOM. Nowadays we have other methods of dealing with witches—less crude perhaps, but just as nasty.

SARAH. What would *you* think of such a person?

TOM. Me? I should think she was a freak.

SARAH. It would be horrible to be a freak. One couldn't love a freak, I suppose.

TOM. Not a decent, normal man, I should think.

SARAH. What loneliness!

TOM. My dear, you're trembling. (*Gently.*) Mrs. Moonlight, please don't be morbid. Do you think *you're* a freak just because people still pay you compliments on your looks at the ripe old age of twenty-eight?

SARAH. You hear them talking more than I, Tom. Is it always compliments?

TOM. Well, mostly.

SARAH. Mostly?

TOM. Yes—very often.

SARAH. Edith didn't seem to think so.

TOM. Edith's jealous.

SARAH. No, she's not. She never has been that. I've heard murmurs myself—already—although I am only twenty-eight. They think it's odd. (*Barely above a whisper.*) So do I. I know I looked like this five years ago; and ten years ago. Once upon a time I used to pray above all things that I should never grow older, look older. I think that was wicked, as well as silly. I thought you'd stop loving me if I did. Now I think you'll stop if I don't. (*She has worked herself up almost to a pitch of wildness.*)

TOM. But you will, darling; of course you'll look older in time.

SARAH. You'd rather I did?

TOM. Of course I would. There's quite enough that's miraculous about my wife without that.

SARAH. (*Trying to control herself.*) It sounds foolish when I talk about it to you; but not when I'm alone. Sometimes it's frightened me till I could hardly help screaming. Like a nightmare that's always there. I wake up in the night crying quietly, and I've wanted to wake you. It's at the back of my mind always—always rasping, fretting, scratching at my brain—till sometimes I feel I'm going mad and can't stand it any longer. You see, it's growing stronger, not weaker; every year for years, ever since Jane was born. (*Hardly above a whisper.*) I don't know what's going to happen. One day it will drive—drive me to—

TOM. (*Comforting her.*) Silly Mrs. Moonlight!

SARAH. Do you think I'm just fanciful?

TOM. Certainly I do. And you always were. It's much too early for *you* to jump to conclusions. Ninon de l'Enclos kept her looks long after twenty-eight. *She* looked young when she was seventy.

SARAH. Poor lady. How tired she must have felt! Tom.

TOM. Yes, dear.

SARAH. You'll always believe, whatever happens, that I love you, won't you?

TOM. Yes, dear; but nothing can or will or shall happen. In fact, I promise you that in the morning you will look a hundred and two. There, will that satisfy you?

BIG LAKE [1]

by

LYNN RIGGS

LLOYD *and* BETTY *are very young. They live in Indian Territory, now Oklahoma, in the year 1906. He is tall, dark and sensitive looking. She is very fair. The occasion is a school picnic at Big Lake. They have come ahead of the others and have borrowed a boat from a man who has committed a murder. At the time of this scene he is scheming to place suspicion on Lloyd.*

After a moment, LLOYD *and* BETTY *enter from the left.* BETTY *goes hurriedly toward the boat and is about to get in.* LLOYD *stops.*

LLOYD. Betty— (*She turns.*) Betty, they jist went. I guess they're ready t' eat, now—

BETTY. (*Shaken.*) I don't keer—

LLOYD. Aw, you mustn't be excited about nuthin'—

BETTY. I ain't excited.

LLOYD. Yes, you air, too. I c'n tell the way you act. You see— they wuzn't nuthin'—

BETTY. No—

LLOYD. Nuthin' a-tall. They uz nice folks. (*Trying to reassure her.*) Funny place t' be a-livin' in though—buried under the ground, like. Looks like it ud be damp s' close to the lake. But they uz nice folks. Nice womern. The man uz all right. Kind of a lumberin' kinda man—'thout no talk—but kindhearted. Didden he loan us the boat?

BETTY. Yes—

LLOYD. Didden he give us the oars? Shore he did! Well?—

BETTY. Le's go on the lake now, Lloyd—

LLOYD. Shore! We'll go, all right. I said we'd go. (*He goes toward her. She gets in the boat. A burst of song and laugh-*

[1] Copyright, 1927, by Lynn Riggs; 1927, by Samuel French.

ter comes from the picnickers some distance away. He raises his head.) Betty, listen! They're gettin' breakfast ready, I guess.

BETTY. I don't want none.

LLOYD. All right, I ain't s' hungry. But I'm jist wonderin'— wh'er we hadn't oughter let 'em know we've come. I told Bud Bickel we uz comin' early by ourselves. They might wonder about us—or wait fer us.

BETTY. They won't wait. They're startin' a f'ar.

LLOYD. Smoke's a-rizin' good. It's a-comin' off the ground an' rizin' up like a cloud. We oughter be thar. Miss Meredith might worry about us.

BETTY. She wouldn't worry about us. She wouldn't worry about no one. Please, Lloyd, le's go out on the lake—a little while, just fer a little—

LLOYD. (*Anxiously.*) Whut is it?

BETTY. Nuthin'—

LLOYD. Tell me—

BETTY. (*With sudden passion.*) Oh, *them!* That cabin! Them people! That man! I'm afeard of him, he's a part of these woods here! He's part of this. I don't like it. It's busy, busy a-doin' sump'n I can't understand! They ain't nuthin' clear t' me. Why'd he look at me that a-way? Why'd he want me t' borry a coat t' keep warm? Why'd he stir up the f'ar—fer *me?* Why did he?

LLOYD. Why, Betty, he uz only bein' nice t' you. He liked you. People like you—you're sweet, you're purty—

BETTY. No. It ain't that! It's sump'n else. I don't understand it. I'm afeard. I'm too young. It's wrong t' be young—

LLOYD. Betty! Why, here—

BETTY. His eyes a-burnin'— His teeth—like a animal's—

LLOYD. Betty!

BETTY. He's a *part* o' these woods here! He b'longs here. I don't. I don't b'long here. You don't. We're too young. They's sump'n goin' on—sump'n mean—sump'n awful— It ain't fer us t' be part of. We got to git away—

LLOYD. We'll go on the lake.

BETTY. Oh, yes, we'll go on the lake! (*Thoughtfully.*) Nen whur'll we go to?

LLOYD. *Acrost* the lake—or down to the other end. We c'n git a snack t' eat at Binghams. We'll do that 'n' then row home. We won't come back here t' the woods if you don't want to—

BETTY. We couldn't jist stay—in the middle of the lake—awhile?

LLOYD. Course we could—fer a while. But you'd be hungry. You'd be cold out thar too after a while. The wind blows—

BETTY. (*Fearfully.*) All around the lake, everwhur, they's woods. The lake goes out—'n' it's clear thar and bright—but it teches the woods everwhur at the edges. Oh! They ain't no place t' go to! The lake—it teches the woods—it's a *part* of the woods! (*She sinks down.*)

LLOYD. (*Kneeling.*) No! No, it ain't, Betty. You're jist upset. It'll be nice out thar. It'll be clear an' bright. Mebbe it'll be warm. We'll stay as long's you want to. You mustn't be this a-way, don't you see, Betty? Oh, I know—you're jist upset, you've saw things you don't understand. You've been skeered. It's all right now. You mustn't think everything's mixed up like this—like these woods. Out there—look at it—look at the lake! (*Breathlessly.*) Sun techin' it. Little waves startin' in the wind, breakin' here on the bank in ripples. Trees—willers leanin' down like they uz prayin' at the edges. I wish I could be a lake. I wish I could be that big, that deep! I wish I could be ketchin' the sun like it—an' sparklin' an' singin'—an' never afeard o' nuthin'—jist a-settin' thar quiet in the sunshine—a-lookin' up at the sky, a-lookin' up at the sun—

BETTY. (*Looking at him.*) You make it nice—

LLOYD. No, 'tain't me—

BETTY. You make it nicer'n it is—

LLOYD. No. It looks that a-way t' me.

BETTY. It's that a-way t' me, too—

LLOYD. (*Relieved.*) Betty—

BETTY. When you say it. You make things nicer'n they air—
LLOYD. No, I make 'em the *way* they air.
BETTY. An' the lake?—
LLOYD. It's a deep pool—
BETTY. It's quiet.
LLOYD. It moves when the wind moves. It holds the sun. It's a cup with gold in it—
BETTY. And dawn—
LLOYD. An' sunset, and shadders, and starlight, an' the moon burnin' red. Come on, why'd we stay on the bank? We'll go out— (*He climbs into the boat.*)
BETTY. Yes.

FOR SERVICES RENDERED [1]

by

W. SOMERSET MAUGHAM

EVA, *a woman of thirty-nine years, was engaged to a man who was killed in the war. Since then she has devoted herself to the care of her blind brother. She is thin, haggard and on the verge of a nervous breakdown. She has fallen in love with* COLLIE STRATTON, *an ex-naval officer who runs a garage, principally because he is the only eligible man in the small English village. He has just learned that because he post-dated checks when his account was overdrawn, he must go to jail.*

COLLIE, *sinking into a chair, buries his face in his hands; but hearing the door open he looks up and pulls himself together.* EVA *comes in.*

EVA. Oh, I beg your pardon. I was looking for my bag. I didn't know anyone was here.
COLLIE. I was just going.

[1] From *For Services Rendered*, by W. Somerset Maugham. Copyright, 1932, 1933. Reprinted by permission of Doubleday, Doran & Company, Inc.

EVA. Please don't. I won't disturb you.

COLLIE. What are you talking about? Surely you can come into your own dining room.

EVA. I wasn't speaking the truth. I knew you were here and my bag's upstairs. I heard father go. I wanted to see you. I'm so frightfully anxious.

COLLIE. What about?

EVA. Everyone knows you're in difficulties. Father let fall a hint at luncheon. I knew he was seeing you this afternoon.

COLLIE. It's kind of you to bother, Evie. I've had rather a rough passage, but at all events I know where I am now.

EVA. Can nothing be done?

COLLIE. Not very much, I'm afraid.

EVA. Won't you let me help you?

COLLIE. (*With a smile.*) My dear, how can you?

EVA. It's only a matter of money, isn't it?

COLLIE. Only is good.

EVA. I've got a thousand pounds that my godmother left me. It's invested and I've always dressed myself on the interest. I could let you have that.

COLLIE. I couldn't possibly take money from you. It's out of the question.

EVA. Why? If I want to give it you.

COLLIE. It's awfully generous of you, but . . .

EVA. (*Interrupting.*) You must know how frightfully fond I am of you.

COLLIE. It's very nice of you, Evie. Besides, your father would never hear of it.

EVA. It's my own money. I'm not a child.

COLLIE. Can't be done, my dear.

EVA. Why shouldn't I buy an interest in your garage? I mean, then it would be just an investment.

COLLIE. Can you see your father's face when you suggested it? It looked all right when I bought it. Things were booming then. But the slump has killed it. It isn't worth a bob.

EVA. But surely if you can get more capital you can afford to wait till times get better?

COLLIE. Your father doesn't think much of me as it is. He'd think me a pretty mean skunk if he thought I'd induced you to put your money into an insolvent business.

EVA. You keep talking of father. It's nothing to do with him. It's you and I that are concerned.

COLLIE. I know you're a damned good sort and you're always going out of your way to do things for people, but there are limits. Perhaps you'll want to get married one of these days, and then you'll find your thousand pounds devilish useful.

EVA. I shall never have a better use for it than to give it to someone who means so much to me as you do.

COLLIE. I'm awfully sorry, God knows I want the money, but I really can't take it from anyone like you.

EVA. I thought you liked me.

COLLIE. I like you very much. You're a jolly good friend.

EVA. I thought perhaps some day we might be more than friends. (*There is a moment's silence. She is very nervous, but forces herself to go on.*) After all, if we were engaged, it would be very natural that I should come to the rescue when you were in a hole.

COLLIE. But we're not engaged.

EVA. Why shouldn't we pretend to be? Just for a little while, I mean. Then I could lend you the money and father would help you to get straight.

COLLIE. Oh, my dear, that's absurd. That's the sort of thing they do in novels. You mustn't be so romantic.

EVA. You could always break it off when you got straight.

COLLIE. That's not a very pretty rôle you're asking me to play.

EVA. (*In a husky voice.*) Perhaps when you got used to the idea you wouldn't want to break it off.

COLLIE. My dear, what on earth ever put such an idea in your head?

EVA. You're alone and I'm alone. There's no one in the world that cares twopence for either of us.

COLLIE. Oh, what nonsense. Your family's devoted to you. They depend on you so enormously. Why, the whole house centres round you.

EVA. I want to get away. I'm so unhappy here.

COLLIE. I can't believe that. You're just nervous and run down. I daresay you want a bit of change.

EVA. You won't understand. How can you be so cruel?

COLLIE. I'm not cruel. I'm awfully grateful to you.

EVA. I can't say any more than I have. It's so humiliating.

COLLIE. I'm dreadfully sorry. I don't want to hurt your feelings.

EVA. After all, I'm not so old as all that. Plenty of men have wanted to marry me.

COLLIE. I don't doubt that for a minute. I'm quite convinced that one of these days you'll find someone that you really like, and I'm sure you'll make him a perfectly grand wife. (*She begins to cry and he looks at her with troubled eyes.*) I'm sorry. (*She does not answer, and quietly he leaves the room.*)

ACCENT ON YOUTH [1]

by

SAMSON RAPHAELSON

STEVEN GAYE, *a successful playwright, has decided to go to Finland on a long holiday, giving up all plans for his new play. He is, in spite of his conceit, a very attractive man. His secretary,* LINDA BROWN, *has just been discharged.*

LINDA.—Now we're through—aren't we?

GAYE. Why—it looks that way.

LINDA. You're no longer my employer.

GAYE. No.

LINDA. And I'm no longer your—secretary.

GAYE. Right.

LINDA. We're two human beings together.

GAYE. Yes, Linda.

LINDA. A man and a woman.

GAYE. A man and a woman.

LINDA. (*Putting the check in her purse.*) Well—before I say good-bye, I want you to know that I love you.—I want you to know that the three years and two months I've spent with you have been the most wonderful, painful, happiest years I've ever had or hope to have. You hardly knew I was on earth—but you've given me more than you could have given your wife, or any other woman, or your friends, or your audiences. I had you when you were alone.—You've spoiled every man I know for me. You did that in the first month. I don't think I'll ever forget a single look of your face, a single word you said. . . . You've done a terrible thing: you opened my eyes and my heart—and you never touched me. It hurt—every bit of it hurt—how could it not hurt, it was so beautiful!— And if you think I can walk out of this house quietly— that you can smile me away with money and a few dresses —if you think I can walk out of here without wanting to kill you, without wanting to cut my initials into every day you're going to live, you're crazy. . . . Good-bye—and *try* to forget me! (*She starts out.*)

GAYE. Hey! (*He rushes over and takes her by the arm. He leads her slowly back into the room. She is sobbing. Looking at her very thoughtfully.*) Let me look at you. (*Quietly.*) You strange creature. . . . You lovely creature. (*She makes a move. He takes her arm.*) Don't go away!—let me look at you some more. I'm not patronizing you. I'm *seeing* you. You're grand! . . . If I only were thirty-five, or forty, instead of—fifty-one . . . What do you want of me, Linda?

LINDA. Nothing.

GAYE. That's not true.

LINDA. (*Breaking.*) I know it's not true.

GAYE. What do you want of me, Linda?

LINDA. I don't know. . . . Everything. . . . Anything.

GAYE. Sit down. (*He gently leads her to the sofa.*) Of course. . . . Of course. . . . Most natural thing in the world.—Where do you live, Linda?

LINDA. West Tenth Street.

GAYE. Apartment?

LINDA. Yes.

GAYE. And your parents are dead.—You went to college or something, didn't you?

LINDA. Three years.

GAYE. (*To himself.*) Why, certainly. A girl like that—I come into her life—and it happens. Suddenly, like a banquet, she gets Broadway, literature, personalities, and me. . . . Linda, I know you won't believe it—but you'll get over this.

LINDA. (*Despairingly.*) Will I?

GAYE. Yes, you will. You're young, and you made yourself ready. The world is full of fascinating people—much more fascinating than I am.

LINDA. You know that isn't so.

GAYE. (*Slowly.*) I suppose there's something in what you say. . . . (*Turns to her with curiosity.*) Am I physically attractive?

LINDA. Yes.

GAYE. Funny, when you get right down to it, I can't think offhand of a man—you know—who *could* make you forget me. I'm beginning to see what a spot you're in! I *am* a unique combination—witty, sensitive, imaginative, worldly, gay—and yet with a feeling for tragedy. . . . And I know myself too well, I've been around too much, to deny that I'm charming.

LINDA. You're wonderful.

GAYE. Demmit—I know I am! . . . But, Linda, my sweet, I don't love you—I don't love anybody.

LINDA. (*Suffering.*) I know that. You don't have to tell me—I know that.

GAYE. And if I did love you. Suppose, for the sake of argument, I fell in love with you. It would be worse. Picture a man of fifty-one—why, it's like the situation in "Old Love" . . . (*He stops, completely smitten with an idea.*) Oh, my God. . . . (*He turns to her, staring at her but not seeing her—springs up.*) Linda— (*Excitedly.*) Get your notebook. (*In a daze, she obeys, picking up notebook and pencil. . . . He walks up and down the room in great excitement. She sits, waiting for dictation.*)

LINDA. Ready.

GAYE. (*Thrilled, boyish.*) . . . Linda, this is marvelous! (*He comes over to her.*) How can I ever repay you? Do you realize what you've done for me? (*She looks up at him, bewildered.*) Angel—you've saved my play!

I LOVE AN ACTRESS [1]

by

LASZLO FODOR

GEORGE *is a charming, impetuous young man with a magnetic personality. For three months he has followed* EVA SANDOR *about town, but until now has never spoken to her.* EVA *is a successful actress, glamorous yet demure. The scene is a department store in Buda-Pesth.*

GEORGE *approaches* EVA *three steps. She looks at wrist watch.* GEORGE *swallows, then one step closer.* EVA *fixes watch strap.* GEORGE *one step closer.* EVA *winds watch.*

GEORGE. Please! You really don't notice me or just don't want to notice me! (EVA *lifts watch to her ear.*) Why? Was I too aggressive? (EVA *straightens her foot. Takes cigarette and table lighter. When cigarette is in mouth.*) I follow you always at a respectable distance. You can't resent that! (*She exhales a puff; puts lighter down; crosses her foot.*) Forgive me. The street is a public place. So is the store. Anyone may come in here. Do not be angry with me. I can't help it! (EVA *takes a puff of cigarette, long draw.*) Believe me, I also find this terrible! But what am I to do? (EVA *puts cigarette down; picks up bag in lap; opens bag; vanity case out; looks at herself.*) It is not my fault that you are so beautiful! (EVA *powders her face during speech.*) If you accept the advantages your beauty gives you—you must bear with its disadvantages as well. One who is so beautiful must stand for the consequences. (*Powder back, lipstick out, rouging lips.*) I have no other sin but that I bought a ticket to the theatre one night— *you* are responsible for the rest! (*Puts vanity case in bag and shuts bag; bag down; sits back in chair.*) So everything is futile. You are not going to notice me? (EVA *takes off hat; shakes her head.*) You do not want to notice me? . . . (GEORGE *starts left and stops.* EVA *rises and crosses left to mirror.* GEORGE *crosses to right.* EVA *returns to table.*) And really, believe me, I do not want very much— (EVA *combs one side.*) A glance is enough for me—a smile—with which you signify that you have noticed me and that my presence is not too obnoxious— (EVA *fixes other side of hair.*) Maddening! The great actress, who cannot smile! (EVA *fixes her hair with both hands.*) Although—a smile—a smile would give me energy to continue—a smile would last me three months, and would enable me to go on—to follow you further, like a shadow—from house to house, from street to street, from store to store— (EVA *crosses to chair; sits, takes bag, puts comb back in bag, crosses knees. Bag down. Pause.*) How beautiful it is when we are shopping—and if you knew how much I have bought on your account— (EVA *looks straight ahead.*) A box of hairpins— (*Taking each article out of his pockets.*) I bought them at the hairdresser's, where you had your hair done. (*Left coat pocket.*) Shoestrings— (*Right coat pocket.*) from the shoemaker's. Scented soap— (*Inside pocket.*) —from the perfumer's— Ping-pong ball— (*Left pants' pocket.*) —from the sporting goods store— . . . (*Puts ping-pong ball back in pocket. Faces* EVA.) So it is all useless? (EVA *starts putting hat on.*) I understand— (GEORGE *turns and walks right a few steps, then turns to* EVA.) But I put all blame on you. You will be the cause if I should do something rash! Because everything has limits —and if you so stubbornly and steadily refuse to notice me, then a moment must come when you will be forced to notice—then you will understand what an embittered young man is ready to do—

PETTICOAT FEVER [1]

by

MARK REED

DASCOM DINSMORE *is the wireless operator at the northern-most station at Labrador. He is a young Englishman, well educated and very attractive.* ETHEL CAMPION *and* SIR JAMES, *her fiancé, flying to Montreal, have missed their course in a storm and have taken shelter in* DASCOM'S *house.* DASCOM *is very sincere though rather childish in his very apparent delight at seeing a beautiful woman.*

DASCOM *immediately reappears, crosses to* ETHEL'S *door, makes a false knock with open hand, then, screwing up his courage, actually knocks.*

ETHEL. What is it?
DASCOM. Miss Campion, I advise you not to stay in there. You might get a chill.
(*She comes out. His face lights up.*)
ETHEL. I think I will return to the fire, if you don't mind.
DASCOM. Not at all (*He stands at extreme end of fireplace,*

rising to his toes, embarrassed; yet aglow with excitement.)
Is . . . is there anything I can get you?
ETHEL. No, thanks.
DASCOM. Would you like some tea?
ETHEL. No, thanks.
DASCOM. Whiskey and soda . . . without the soda?
ETHEL. No, please.
DASCOM. I'll get you some hot soup. (*Forgetting the soup, he sits and gazes at her, sighing rapturously.*)
ETHEL. I beg your pardon . . .
DASCOM. I beg yours.
ETHEL. I thought you spoke.
DASCOM. No. I . . . I'm trying to think of something adequate to the occasion.
ETHEL. (*Restless under his scrutiny.*) Well, for heaven's sake, hurry up about it!
DASCOM. It's awfully cosy to have you here.
ETHEL. I imagine you must get frightfully bored.
DASCOM. Not at all. At times it's frightfully exciting here. Why only last Sunday, we had 2,700 miles of wind.
ETHEL. That's a lot of wind.
DASCOM. Isn't it? (*He sees long ash on her cigarette. Gallantly he flicks it into fireplace and returns cigarette with a bow.*)
ETHEL. (*Making a desperate effort at conversation.*) I am sure you and Sir James will hit it off. (*She moves chair away. He moves stool nearer.*) He likes rough life . . . the sea, the mountains. He has a ranch of his own in Saskatchewan. You'll like him. He is a man's man, too.
DASCOM. I'm not a man's man.
ETHEL. Surely you can't be much of a woman's man, up here?
DASCOM. I do labor under difficulties. You're the first beautiful woman I've seen in two years.
ETHEL. Anyone would look attractive to you.
DASCOM. Oh, no. (*Indicates pictures on wall.*) I have kept

my standards high. You're beautiful. Stake my last pound on it.

ETHEL. That will be quite unnecessary.

DASCOM. I'll bet you five pounds you are beautiful. You on—?

ETHEL. I think right now is an excellent time for me to make an announcement. (*She extends her left hand for him to see the ring on it.*)

DASCOM. Sir James?

ETHEL. Yes.

DASCOM. (*Rising sadly.*) I'll get you some soup. (*At door, he hesitates, then comes back.*) Pardon, I forgot to congratulate you. *Sir James* will be very happy. (*Lost again in contemplation of her beauty, he sits.*) You must have been very unhappy at home. (*She tries to give him a haughty look. A pause—then gently.*) After all, engagement is a very frail institution, isn't it? Very frail.

ETHEL. I was going to ask you: Is there a rector in the neighborhood?

DASCOM. (*With profound satisfaction.*) Not within one hundred miles.

ETHEL. Really?

DASCOM. And I am not a Justice of the Peace, I'm happy to say—

ETHEL. You see, Sir James didn't wish to be married on the boat. He loathed the captain because he used the Culbertson system.

DASCOM. I'm horribly out of it—is that a new kind of marriage?

ETHEL. No, contract. When we landed at St. Johns, it seemed only a few hours' fly to Montreal . . . and we were in a frightful hurry.

DASCOM. Both of you?

ETHEL. Sir James is scheduled to speak three nights this week.

DASCOM. Good! I'll be delighted to listen to him.

LADY OF LETTERS

by

TURNER BULLOCK

ADELAIDE *is the kind of person who is always in trouble because of something she has said or done unconsciously. "Her manner is utterly simple, childlike and direct without a trace of silliness, affectation, coquetry or vanity." She is married to a professor.* RICHARD *is a young author. While on his way to Mexico, his car is hit by* ADELAIDE'S. *After a quarrel his employer leaves without him. He is broke and utterly disheartened.*

ADELAIDE. Did you get your luggage out of the car before she left?
RICHARD. (*Pointing to a small satchel.*) I got that.
ADELAIDE. (*Eyeing it.*) Is it your overnight case?
RICHARD. No.-. . . It's a novel.
ADELAIDE. Ohh. . . .
RICHARD. A superb novel—four hundred and eighty-five pages long—and no one will ever read it.
ADELAIDE. (*Tremendously impressed.*) I'll read it—if you'll let me.
RICHARD. Oh no you won't. The novel that nobody ever read —that's what it'll be. It's been rejected by every publisher in the country! It's all mine—flesh of my flesh—bone of my bone. . . . (*Leans back and covers face with his hands.*)
ADELAIDE. (*Approaches case with awe. Picks it up reverently.*) What are you going to do with it?
RICHARD. Nothing.
ADELAIDE. Aren't you going to try and have it published?
RICHARD. Not any more.
ADELAIDE. Why not?
RICHARD. I told you. They've all rejected it. They never take anything—they write all the books themselves. First you

send it and then you wait and wait and wait and then it comes back and you change it and send it again and wait some more—and so it goes.

ADELAIDE. But then—sometime—it might be accepted.

RICHARD. It might. But I probably won't be here to appreciate it.

ADELAIDE. Where will you be?

RICHARD. Dead, probably.

ADELAIDE. But you aren't sick, are you?

RICHARD. Not more than most people. There are ways of dying other than from sickness.

ADELAIDE. (*Appalled.*) You mean—you'd kill yourself?

RICHARD. (*Amused.*) I might. It wouldn't make much difference—at the moment.

ADELAIDE. But you mustn't do that!

RICHARD. Why not? (*Suddenly disgusted.*) Oh what's the use of all this talk! You don't understand.

ADELAIDE. (*Sadly.*) That's what people always say to me. I *might* understand. (*Pause.*) What will become—

RICHARD. Please now! Stop asking questions.

ADELAIDE. I was only going to say—what will become of your novel?

RICHARD. What does it matter? There are more novels than most people have time to read.

ADELAIDE. But just the same—

RICHARD. (*Angrily.*) Oh if you're so worried, why don't you take it and publish it yourself?

ADELAIDE. (*Enchanted.*) Can I really do that!

RICHARD. Why not?

ADELAIDE. I can really take and publish it . . . ?

RICHARD. (*With a wave of disgust.*) You can even be the author of it. You can put your own name on it—mine never brought it any luck— You can do whatever you like with it—

ADELAIDE. (*Awed.*) You mean that? (*Quickly.*) I'll pay you—if you let me have it. . . .

RICHARD. (*Suddenly realizing she is serious.*) You'll pay

me. . . . (*Goes into paroxysms of laughter.*) . . . It would be magnificent, if . . .

ADELAIDE. Well, if you're not going to use it—*somebody* ought to. . . .

RICHARD. (*Suddenly serious himself.*) What would you pay for it. . . .

ADELAIDE. Well, I have five hundred dollars all my own in a nice little bank in Chicago. Would that be enough?

RICHARD. (*To whom the sum is a fortune.*) Five hundred —you'd give me five hundred dollars? For that pile of paper?

ADELAIDE. I'd give you more if I had it. . . .

RICHARD. Well, I—oh this is preposterous. What in the world do you want with it?

ADELAIDE. Well—Gilbert has a book and everybody else— is so smart and knows so many things. . . . (*Wistfully.*) If I could have one too—just for my very own— (*Brightening.*) And you'd have a little money—so you wouldn't have to kill yourself—at least not right away. . . .

RICHARD. Oh, I couldn't do it. You'd be wasting your money. I told you nobody wants the book.

ADELAIDE. I want it—even if I just keep it here myself. Gilbert says I always waste my money anyway.

RICHARD. You'd only get into trouble. Why, you haven't even read it.

ADELAIDE. I'm sure it's good—if you wrote it.—Four hundred and eighty-five pages—

RICHARD. (*Bitterly.*) My public—my first admirer!

ADELAIDE. I'll give you the money—right now! (*Crosses to the desk.*)

RICHARD. (*Following her.*) Wait a minute! You don't know anything about me. How do you know I won't take your money, spend it and then come back?

ADELAIDE. If you spend the money and then change your mind and want your book back, you can have it.

RICHARD. You needn't worry, I won't. (*She takes out her check book.*) What bank is it on?

ADELAIDE. It's my little bank. Right around the corner from where I lived in Chicago. Boulevard Branch. Awfully nice people there.

RICHARD. Wait a minute. Maybe it would be a good idea if you made out five checks. They'll be easier to cash and I can cash them as I need them. I needn't carry all the money around with me at once.

ADELAIDE. Yes, you might lose it and then you wouldn't have any more. All right, five checks. (*She tears out five checks and places them all in a line.*)

RICHARD. Each for one hundred dollars.

ADELAIDE. (*Writes.*) May 4, 1934. Mr. Richard—

RICHARD. Mays.

ADELAIDE. M-a-z-e?

RICHARD. No, M-a-y-s—

ADELAIDE. (*Starts to fill out checks muttering*—) Richard Mays—Richard Mays— (*Chuckling as she writes.*) If the book is ever published, I'll bet Gilbert'll say I'm a pretty smart little woman, after all. (*Muttering as she fills out checks*—) One hundred dollars—one hundred dollars— He'll say I saved a work of literature from oblivion—like somebody I once read about in a footnote— (MAYS *looks at her with commiseration. She hands him the checks.*) There!

RICHARD. This one isn't signed. (*Hands back a check.*)

ADELAIDE. (*Taking it gaily.*) Oh, of course— (*Muttering as she signs.*) Adelaide Willifer—such a long name—

RICHARD. (*Taking his script from bag.*) And mind if you send it out you must take my name off the manuscript!

ADELAIDE. (*Giving him the check.*) You really think I should?

RICHARD. I insist— You see— (*Rather vaguely.*) I don't want to get into any trouble with my creditors—

ADELAIDE. Then you'd really want me to put my name on it?

RICHARD. Why not? It may bring it luck—

ADELAIDE. (*Elated.*) All right, then I'll do it. (*Reading the title page in a hushed voice.*) "New Destinies." What does it mean?

RICHARD. You'd better find out for yourself. It'd be a good idea for you to read the book anyway.

ADELAIDE. (*Absently.*) Yes, of course.

RICHARD. (*With irony.*) And whatever you don't like, you can change to suit yourself.

ADELAIDE. Oh, that would be lovely.

RICHARD. (*Taking up case and preparing to go.*) And I advise you not to let anyone connected with the college read it—at least not until it's published.

ADELAIDE. (*Lost in rapture.*) I won't—

RICHARD. It might make a fuss. (*He realizes it is useless to say more.*) Goodbye. (*He goes through the hall—chuckling to himself. Adelaide immediately claps the pages to her bosom. She then begins to read the first page. Her brow makes little furrows. She then takes to reading the numbers on the final pages.*)

ADELAIDE. . . . 485—486—487! About a dollar a page. That's not so bad.

THE BRIDE THE SUN SHINES ON [1]

by

WILL COTTON

PSYCHE *is "a normally bright, happy, well-bred girl." She is very fond of* ALFRED, *whom she is about to marry. But she is angry because she believes* HUBERT, *for whom she has always had a great affection, has paid too much attention to the local siren.* HUBERT *is a musician, erratic, well-poised, attractive. Loving his freedom, he went away when he found himself falling in love with* PSYCHE. *She does not know this.*

PSYCHE. (*Still on sofa right.*) You know, I wouldn't be surprised if this wedding finally took place.

HUBERT. (*At foot of stairs.*) It may.

PSYCHE. Hubert—

HUBERT. (*Who has started up stairs.*) Yes?

PSYCHE. It was wonderful of you to come just to play at my wedding.

HUBERT. It was.

PSYCHE. Hubert—why do you avoid me?

HUBERT. (*Descends.*) But I don't. What an idea!

PSYCHE. Then why do you run away as soon as we are left alone in a room together?

HUBERT. (*Crosses to left center.*) Oh, don't be silly.

PSYCHE. Silly! You aren't even civil to me.

HUBERT. Should one expect that from a member of one's family?

PSYCHE. You're not a member of my family.

HUBERT. (*Crosses to right, left of sofa.*) With all your bright young friends around, I've felt like an uncle. Just a superfluous creature who has known you all your life, seen you through scarlet fever, mumps and measles, and so with whom a moment alone must be inevitably tedious.

PSYCHE. There's no danger of that—unless you have changed— We were always friends before.

HUBERT. We still are. Just the same as we have been—as long as I remember.

PSYCHE. Then your memory is getting bad. We always used to have some sort of fun together—and now you don't pay any attention to me.

HUBERT. What shall we do? Play house?— I thought you had grown up.

PSYCHE. (*Rises.*) You're so aloof. I noticed it the minute you came yesterday— Oh, what's the use? You keep away for months and months all over Europe, and then when you do get back you act as though you hated us. No! I don't mean that. (*Puts arms around his shoulders.*) I'm sorry.

HUBERT. (*Crosses to center.*) Now you keep off! Don't forget you're engaged to be married.

PSYCHE. (*Drawing away.*) I'm beginning to think men are impossible.

HUBERT. You are growing up. Good Lord! You're not going to cry! (*Crosses to* PSYCHE *right.*)

PSYCHE. (*Crosses to left.*) It's only because I'm tired of this mess!

HUBERT. This what?

PSYCHE. I wish Alfred and I had gone to a Justice of the Peace and had it over with. Why should we have to put up with all this—this "big affair," this "social event," with everybody we ever heard of suddenly coming piling down on us! (*At table, picks up the small package. . . .*) If I see another present, I'll— (*Draws her arm back to hurl the package out of the window.*) I hope it's *glass.*

HUBERT. (*Crosses to left. Picks up package.*) Hey, there! Let me see that.

PSYCHE. Whatever it is, I'm sure to have at least six just like it.

HUBERT. Then chuck it out. Go on! It's only the present *I* sent you. And it's not glass—and I spent *days* finding something I knew you wouldn't have six of.

PSYCHE. You darling!

HUBERT. You'd better look at it first to see if you need be so pleased.

PSYCHE. This is like old times—when you always brought me things—books—

HUBERT. (*An insult.*) Teddy bears.

PSYCHE. Music.

HUBERT. (*Another insult.*) Lollypops!

PSYCHE. All kinds of silly little things.

HUBERT. (*Indignantly.*) I gave you your first motor.

PSYCHE. (*The package now open. She takes out a doll. Gasps. Sees necklace around neck of doll. Takes it off.*) Hubert!! It's lovely! It's jade!! Isn't it? You never brought me anything like this before— You darling!! (*Rises; throws her arms about him.*) You dear—

HUBERT. Don't. (*Crosses down right.*)

PSYCHE. Hubert, you're so cold and distant.

HUBERT. I—I am cold—and I'd *like* to be distant! (*Moves away.*) I'm positively glacial, and I loathe being kissed. Keep away from me. And I'll keep away from you.

PSYCHE. Oh— (*Slowly drops present into the box.*)

HUBERT. I take back what I said a moment ago— You have *not* grown up. You—you—are—eh—

PSYCHE. What?—What am I?

HUBERT. Well—I'd better remind you—you are going to be a bride in an hour.

PSYCHE. I knew that. (*Puts box back on table.*)

HUBERT. Well—you've got to give up going around kissing men, and all that.

PSYCHE. I don't "go around"—and all that. And if you can't be thanked decently for blue jade, I'd better go and dress. (*Crosses to left.*)

HUBERT. It is fifteen minutes past two. (*Crosses to stairs . . .*)

PSYCHE. Don't keep up that master-of-ceremonies pose.

HUBERT. (*Angrily.*) It isn't a pose!! (*Sees* ALFRED. *Changes tone.*) I want to see everything goes off well. . . .

PSYCHE. (*Dryly, as she turns to go.*) We are all very grateful. (*Exit* PSYCHE, *left.*)

THREE CORNERED MOON [1]

by

GERTRUDE TONKONOGY

ELIZABETH RIMPLEGAR *is a girl of about 23. She is a very serious person, but she has no dignity. Being well provided for by her family and having no initiative of her own, she*

[1] Copyright, 1932, 1933, by Gertrude Tonkonogy.

is very bored. She is in love with DONALD, *an eccentric young writer. He is awkward though charming.*

DONALD, *immediately at ease with* ELIZABETH, *throws bouquet carelessly at her. She catches it dexterously but in some confusion.*

ELIZABETH. For Heaven's sakes, what's this!

DONALD. Oh, just some goodies my mother baked for you. (*Crosses to her.*) . . . I have the most marvelous climax for the end of that second part.

ELIZABETII. (*At table. Laughing and unwrapping the package.*) Oh, darling—this is the third time this week you've come with flowers—

DONALD. There's a florist on our block,—I just charge them.

ELIZABETH. I thought you were broke.

DONALD. (*Delightedly.*) But I *am.* As a matter of fact I've been dispossessed again. (*Follows* ELIZABETH *around eagerly as she looks for suitable vase on sideboard.*) I love being dispossessed. It makes me feel as if I have executive ability —running around and telling people to put my etchings down here and my book-cases there and keep my clothes out of the gutter. You ought to try it some time. (*Changing the subject with no apparent break in mood.*) You know that speech of Judith's that I had in Part One—that part where Noel tells her he doesn't love her?

ELIZABETH. Where are you going to live? (*Takes vase from sideboard.*)

DONALD. Didn't you know? I'm coming here. You have plenty of room. . . .

ELIZABETH. (*Crosses to table with vase. To* DONALD.) Of course, there's no telling if you mean it or not. You're as likely to be moving in here as you are to be found sitting on a flagpole. Both are possible. (*Smelling flowers.*) Um. They're beautiful and I love them.

DONALD. (*Going through brief-case and pulling out papers.*) How about me? (ELIZABETH *throws him a kiss.*) . . .

DONALD. (*Runs through papers, mixing them up considerably—dropping several of them. . . .* DONALD *comes to* ELIZABETH *with one paper in right hand—holding sheaf of others in left.*) That speech, dear—that chapter's the wrong place for it. I get a much better effect by having her walk out without a word.

ELIZABETH. (*Looking at paper.*) Uh-huh. She's too moved. (*Crossing right to sofa, looking at manuscript.*) What did you do, though, with the speech you had in here originally? Darling, this is good. (*Reads a few lines to herself.*)

DONALD. (*Crosses to her.*) Oh, I took it out and used it for the climax to Part One. (*Starts walking up and down the room.*) I was up all night with it. About four o'clock I came down here and stood in front of the house but your room was dark.

ELIZABETH. (*Crossing.*) I'm peculiar that way—I like a nap between eleven at night and nine in the morning.

DONALD. (*Smiling tenderly. Below her.*) Something I could never understand about you. (*Stares at her thoughtfully.*)

ELIZABETH. (*Softly—knowing him well.*) What, dearest? (*Sits on arm of sofa.*)

DONALD. If I stand very still and just look at you, I can remember how I felt when I was writing that end part. I kept weeping and weeping and I wrote so fast. I wrote soft and—you know—full of sunlight— (*She nods.*) But there's a recurrent ominous beat in it—first it's faint like a dropping tear—but later it pounds more and more furiously like rainy, thunderous music— (*She is listening to him quietly.*) Ugly sounding phrase, isn't it? I wonder if I write as badly as I talk.

ELIZABETH. (*She shakes her head chidingly.*) Come here, rainy, thunderous one. You know perfectly well you write like a tree on fire. How are you going to do the third part?

DONALD. (*He takes her hands—draws her to the love seat.*) . . . I love you. (*They sit on sofa. He puts his arm around her.*) . . . (*Rises, crosses to table.*) That . . . novel of mine. It's rotten. I don't know what I was so excited about a minute ago. Oh, Elizabeth. (*Wretchedly.*) It's hollow—falling to pieces— I can't get it to go right.

ELIZABETH. Listen here, crazy, if you were in such a blazing turmoil last night, it must be good. That's the way good stuff is written.

DONALD. (*Crosses to chair by fireplace.*) I know. I know. Maybe that part is good—but, . . . I know I could never do it again. I couldn't. I simply couldn't. (*Falling dejectedly into the chair.*) I'm a failure.

ELIZABETH. (*Sighing wearily.*) There you go again. You're always this way after you've written a really grand piece. I should think you'd know by now that this mood will pass just as all the others did.

DONALD. (*Miserably.*) You don't know. You don't know what it's like.

ELIZABETH. Come here, darling. (*He comes to her.*) I've never known you to maintain a level plane of emotion for more than twenty-four hours.

DONALD. That's one reason why I admire you so. You're so wonderfully at peace with yourself.

ELIZABETH. (*Bitterly.*) Oh, me.

DONALD. (*Looking up apprehensively.*) Anything wrong?

ELIZABETH. Everything's wrong. I don't know what's happened to me. I was always such a happy little dope. (*Rises, crosses to stairs.*)

DONALD. (*Crosses to her.*) Why, what is it?

ELIZABETH. I'm miserable—miserable. (*Sits on chest.*)

DONALD. (*Sits next to her.*) You, miserable! Tell me all about it.

ELIZABETH. I don't know exactly. Life's turned sour on me. Ever since I got out of college. I never told you—you're always on the edge of being unhappy yourself. I felt you needed my good spirits. But for six or seven months now I've been in despair—despair.

DONALD. Honey, I'm all upset. Tell me— Tell me. (*Puts arms about her. . . .*)

ELIZABETH. It's such a queer thing. I don't know how to begin. And yet I have a feeling it's sort of natural. . . . I suppose a lot of young people get this way. It's a sort of weltschmertz. I've read about it—but I never knew how real a thing it was till it hit me. I hate everything that goes with life—all its people—all the things it's got to offer.

DONALD. All its people—yes. People give me gooseflesh—except you and you're not people. . . . What started you thinking this way? . . .

ELIZABETH. When I got out of college. I was always so happy in college. There were so many intelligent things to find out—so many people to talk to—people with grand ideas—grand ideals— . . .

DONALD. What about me?

ELIZABETH. I have this dreadful feeling that from now on a person just makes the best of things and grows old. Nothing will ever be the way it was when I was eighteen. That was my zenith when I was eighteen.

DONALD. I had two zeniths.

ELIZABETH. That's right. Spoil my one small pleasure in having had a zenith. . . .

DONALD. You know, you're not exactly a person of wide experience.

ELIZABETH. No. Of course not. But I've read a lot. I know what I can expect. Only more music—more poetry— . . . Nothing new. I think that as I grow older I can only be content—. But I don't want to live if I'm not actively happy. I don't want to compromise. . . . Well—argue with me. Why don't you tell me I'm wrong. I've been hoping some person would come along and show me that I'm absurd. . . .

DONALD. I agree with you so thoroughly. Only—through all *my* miseries there's always been you. Having you, I could never feel the complete emptiness that you feel. You're enough to make up for all the rest.

ELIZABETH. Even when I'm this way?

DONALD. (*Hesitantly.*) I don't know. It's strange to find

you this way. I'm so used to being comforted by you and now— (*Sorrowfully.*) You know if you really loved me, you wouldn't feel that life is empty.

ELIZABETH. Oh, darling. Don't say that. Of course I love you. But I'm not so lopsided as you. No man could so completely fill my life that I could forget everything else. (DONALD *drops his head between his arms.*) Oh darling. Don't. (*Drops on her knees beside him.*)

DONALD. I can't help it. If you're unhappy, I am too. I think if you were miles away and had a toothache, I'd feel it.

ELIZABETH. (*Lifts his head from his lap and looks at him.*) Donald.

DONALD. What, dear.

ELIZABETH. I wonder what you'd think of an idea I have.

DONALD. What?

ELIZABETH. How about getting out of all this?

DONALD. What? Go away? I hate travelling. I never know what to tip porters.

ELIZABETH. No, not that. (*She comes close to him, takes his hand, stares up at him. The room is very still.*) Donald. How about getting out together—how about one grand beautiful exit? How about—

(*He is leaning forward—very wide-eyed—very intent—very frightened.*)

DONALD. (*Frightened whisper.*) What?

ELIZABETH. (*After a pause.*) Suicide.

DONALD. (*Still quieter whisper.*) Suicide!

ELIZABETH. (*Eagerly—now that she's said it.*) Yes—suicide. Suicide together. A beautiful original suicide.

DONALD. (*Cries out in fright. Rises and crosses to fireplace.*) Get away—you're crazy.

ELIZABETH. (*Comes to him again. Intensely—eagerly.*) No, I'm not, Donald. When life's no good for you—the thing to do is to try death. After all there is no other alternative —there's no middle path.

DONALD. Suicide— . . . I haven't thought of that since I flunked algebra.

ELIZABETH. Then think of it now—Donald. If we go on and live—we'll hate each other if life is stale. What is it Schopenhauer says—"the best thing about life is that one has the prerogative of leaving it whenever one wishes"— Well, that's not it exactly—but that's what it means.

DONALD. (*Crosses to her.*) Don't quote. Don't quote. You can make any quotation fit any given situation and still it wouldn't mean a damn thing. (*Thoughtfully.*) How are we to know there's nothing better waiting for us.

ELIZABETH. (*Crosses to center.*) Just tell me this, Donald. What at this moment can you think of that life can give you to make you happy?

DONALD. (*Following her.*) You.

ELIZABETH. (*Softly.*) But if I'm always this way?

DONALD. (*Unhappily.*) Oh, stop it. Stop it. You know how I need you. (*Suddenly decisive.*) Put your arms around me, darling. (*Both embrace.*) Put your arms around me and I'm ready to die. If you're unhappy, I'd rather see you dead, and if you're dead—

ELIZABETH. I was afraid to tell you. I couldn't do it without you.

DONALD. You're sure, dear, that you want to go through with this?

ELIZABETH. Sure? Haven't I been thinking of it for months and months? (*With a sudden change of tone.*) How'll we do it, dear? (*She pulls him down on the floor beside her in front of the sofa, sits cross-legged and they start to plan animatedly as if they were talking of a party.*)

DONALD. Well, let's figure out a good one. I think most suicides are so shabby.

ELIZABETH. And so unoriginal.

DONALD. Ours must be beautiful.

ELIZABETH. And different. . . . Well, now, let's see—what are some of the best methods?

DONALD. Wait now—let me think. . . .

ELIZABETH. Let's go over the tried methods. There's drowning.

DONALD. No, that's no good—I can't swim.

ELIZABETH. That's just the idea—that's fine.

DONALD. No. How could I get into the water so that I could start drowning? What about gas?

ELIZABETH. (*Makes a face.*) Ugh. Smells awful. The smell always makes me nauseous.

DONALD. If you're dying a little thing like nausea isn't going to bother you.

ELIZABETH. I know, but until you get there—ugh.

DONALD. A revolver? . . .

ELIZABETH. Now—that isn't bad—a bullet, yes.

DONALD. It's over before you feel anything, for one thing. . . .

ELIZABETH. A revolver is no good for one reason. We'd put it up and aim and then put it down again. It's like pulling out one of your teeth— The best way—barring dentists, of course, is that business of the string tied to the door so that the first person that comes in does the trick.

DONALD. (*Nodding.*) You'd have to be tied, of course. . . . In other words, we have to rig up a contraption of some sort so that the suicide will be out of our hands once we've put the mechanism in operation.

ELIZABETH. Exactly. Something in the Rube Goldberg tradition. Very complicated and very neat.

DONALD. Wait—let me think—I'm getting an idea. (*Rises. Pulls armchair to corner of room—back to audience, and sits down.*)

THE CURTAIN RISES [1]

by

BENJAMIN M. KAYE

ELSA *is about thirty. Believing that she has no charm and that she is so plain that the romantic side of life is passing her by, she decides to take lessons in acting so she can play a love scene with Vienna's leading actor, Meissinger.* FRANZ *is his understudy. He knows the art of acting so speaks with authority.*

ELSA. I think you'll find that I have already accomplished considerable by myself. I know all the plays of Herr Meissinger by heart.

FRANZ. Well, that—if the Fräulein will permit me—is the least important part of it.

ELSA. But I can't learn to act unless I know the lines, can I?

FRANZ. You cannot learn to act unless you learn a lot of other things first.

ELSA. I don't understand.

FRANZ. (*Rises; crosses left in front of table.*) Will you please rise and walk across the room? (ELSA, *puzzled, rises and walks to window and back center.* FRANZ *watches her.*) No, not like that.

ELSA. What do you mean?

FRANZ. Well, let me explain. You walk—pardon me, Fräulein—without poise—without balance. You don't take much exercise, do you?

ELSA. No.

FRANZ. Well, you will walk one hour a day, rain or shine, one hour steady—with head up, shoulders back, swinging from the hips, like this— You see? (*Illustrates the stride; crosses down right.*)

---

[1] Copyright, 1932, 1933, by Benjamin M. Kaye; 1934, by Samuel French.

ELSA. But I don't like to walk. (*Crosses down to front of table.*)

FRANZ. (*Calmly.*) Herr Meissinger told me that I am to give you lessons—so you will walk one hour every day. At the start I will walk with you to show you how. . . .

ELSA (*Petulantly.*) But I only want to learn to *read* a part.

FRANZ. (*Crosses to couch and picks up newspaper.*) You can *read* a part any time you like—because you have learned how to *read*. But if you want to *act* a part, I must first teach you how to act.

ELSA. (*Crosses to chair right of table.*) But there seems to be so much to do.

FRANZ. (*Crosses to* ELSA.) Ach, that is nothing yet. You will have bending exercises, stretching exercises, practicing facial expressions in front of a mirror, vocal exercises for accent and enunciation.

ELSA. (*More petulantly. Sits right of table.*) I don't think I like your method.

FRANZ. (*Calmly.*) Perhaps not, but you will like my results.

ELSA. (*Very positive.*) Maybe.

FRANZ. (*With a touch of disdain, crosses to* ELSA.) That's the trouble with you amateurs. You think acting is the easiest thing in the world. You don't want to work. (FRANZ *punctuates this sentence by gestures with the folded newspaper.*)

ELSA. (*With anger.*) I'm not an amateur!

FRANZ. (*Still disdainful.*) No? Then what are you?

ELSA. (*Recovering.*) Oh—I'm sorry. I guess I'm just nothing at all.

FRANZ. (*Relenting and trying to ease the situation.*) Now—don't go the other extreme. I only want to see that you start right. Let me show you what I mean. Do you feel like laughing?

ELSA. No.

FRANZ. Good—then laugh.

ELSA. What?

FRANZ. I said laugh! Do you think an actor laughs only

when something is funny? Oh, no. He laughs because it is
written in his part "Laugh." Look, Fräulein—do *I* feel like
laughing at this moment? No. But—I will laugh for you.
(*He starts laughing. First lightly, then louder and louder.*
ELSA *watches him, fascinated. Then she too begins to
laugh.*) . . . So! How is that?

ELSA. (*Controlling her laughter.*) But, Herr Kernmann,
that was so funny!

FRANZ. No, that was not funny. That was acting. Now,
then, shall I cry for you? (*Takes out his handkerchief.*)

ELSA. No, please don't—I begin to understand what you
mean.

FRANZ. If you begin to understand, that is a great deal.
There is much to learn, Fräulein.

THUNDER ON THE LEFT [1]

by

JEAN FERGUSON BLACK

From the novel of the same name by Christopher Morley

On his tenth birthday MARTIN *wishes that he might see
what it is like to be "grown-up." We see him now with the
appearance of a young man although he has the mind and
manners of the boy of ten.* PHYLLIS *is an attractive young
woman. At the moment she is rather harassed over the difficulties of housekeeping at a summer cottage.*

MARTIN *slowly finishes his cake.* PHYLLIS, *at swing, is col-
lecting her writing paraphernalia. She glances casually at*
MARTIN, *whose face is turned from her.*

PHYLLIS. (*Annoyed.*) You cut a piece of that cake, too. You
knew I was saving it.

MARTIN. (*Turning toward her.*) I didn't cut it. The cook gave it to me.

PHYLLIS. (*Astonished, stares at him—then, embarrassed.*) I beg your pardon. (*She takes a step or two toward him.* MARTIN *doesn't rise.*) I just saw the back of you sitting there. I thought you were Mr. Granville, my husband. I'm so sorry.

MARTIN. (*Licking his fingers.*) You mean you're sorry I'm not your husband? (PHYLLIS *is undecided whether or not to resent this.* MARTIN *looks up guilelessly.*) But really, she did give me the cake. You can ask her.

PHYLLIS. (*Smiling, as* MARTIN *licks the last finger.*) Did you enjoy it?

MARTIN. (*Unabashed.*) It was very nice. It tasted good.

PHYLLIS. Don't forget the crumbs on your chin.

MARTIN. (*These he promptly salvages with no trace of self-consciousness.*) Why did you want to save it?

PHYLLIS. I was counting on it for the picnic tomorrow. But it really doesn't matter.

MARTIN. (*Interested.*) A picnic? Can I go? I mean—may I?

PHYLLIS. (*Laughing, a trifle puzzled, comes to sit beside him on the step.*) Have you been very good?

MARTIN. (*Eagerly.*) Yes, I have. Really I have.

PHYLLIS. Then of course you'll have to be invited.

MARTIN. Thank you. I like picnics. Better than anything, almost.

PHYLLIS. Almost? What do you like better?

MARTIN. Christmas—and my mother. I like my mother better than Christmas, of course, and I like you, too. I like you quite a lot. (*He makes this a frank admission.* PHYLLIS *sees he is not flirting. She is puzzled and embarrassed.*)

PHYLLIS. (*Self-conscious effort at conversation.*) Quiet here, isn't it? So restful— My husband and I don't know many of our neighbors. I suppose you feel we're awfully unfriendly—but somehow, when you've been doing the social thing all year— (MARTIN *is watching her earnestly.*) I suppose you're stopping over on the Point. I understood there were quite a few artists over there. I think artists are so interesting. My husband meets quite a few in his business—Advertising, you know. He finds them very interesting. You—*are* an artist, Mr.—

MARTIN. (*Simply.*) I'm Martin, you know.

PHYLLIS. (*It is apparent that this announcement conveys no identification to* PHYLLIS.) Really? Not—eh, *The* Martin? (MARTIN *smiles and nods.*) Why, how honored we are to have so distinguished a neighbor. Mr. Granville and I have admired your work so much.

MARTIN. I'm a good worker. My father always says I am. But I like to play best.

PHYLLIS. (*Laughs.*) I'm afraid we all do.

MARTIN. Do you like to play, too? Will you play with me sometimes?

PHYLLIS. (*Flattered.*) Mr. Martin! I'm an old married woman, the mother of two lively young ladies.

MARTIN. How old?

PHYLLIS. My daughters?

MARTIN. No. You.

PHYLLIS. About how old would you think? Guess.

MARTIN. I can't. Please tell me.

PHYLLIS. Thirty-one.

MARTIN. (*Soberly.*) I bet you've forgotten how to play. I'll have to teach you all over again.

PHYLLIS. (*Affectedly.*) Yes, I'm afraid I have. One does forget how to play. One forgets so much that is real. Life demands it of us.

MARTIN. (*Puzzled.*) Huh?

PHYLLIS. (*Smiling at him.*) I'd like to play with you. Will you teach me,—Martin?

MARTIN. Sure— (*Correcting himself.*) Certainly. When?

PHYLLIS. Tomorrow might be a good time to start, mightn't it? Tomorrow at the picnic?

MARTIN. Yes, that would be a good time.

PHYLLIS. (*A pause.*) Are you down here for the summer or just the week-end, Mr. Martin?

MARTIN. I can stay if you invite me. Have you got room?

PHYLLIS. (*Somewhat disconcerted.*) Why,—yes, indeed. We've plenty of room. I thought perhaps you had made other arrangements.

MARTIN. No. I thought prob'ly you'd invite me. Thank you very much. I'm glad the picnic's tomorrow. There's not so long to wait.

PHYLLIS. Yes— We all look forward to the picnic. Some old friends are coming down for the week-end. They'll be here too. . . .

MARTIN. Is this your house now?

PHYLLIS. No. We're just renting it furnished for the month. We may stay longer. I don't know. It depends— That was another strange thing—the renting of this place. George came down here one day in the spring and took it without my seeing it. There was some reason why he had to sign that afternoon. Anyway, when he came home and started describing the place to me—the location and all—I recognized it immediately. People named Richmond used to live here and summer after summer I practically lived with the Richmond children. They had a boy about my age— His name was Martin, by the way! He had a little sister we called Bunny. Bunny died. She was drowned. (MARTIN *frowns in puzzlement.* PHYLLIS *leans back, surveying the house and grounds.*) I used to think if I could live in this house I'd be perfectly happy.

MARTIN. (*Turning to watch her.*) Are you?

PHYLLIS. Is anyone—ever?

MARTIN. Of course you're not happy. Nobody is after he grows up. (*To himself.*) I knew it.

PHYLLIS. But I don't think children are ever really happy either. I think childhood is tragic. I wouldn't go back to mine for anything.

MARTIN. Wouldn't you, really?

PHYLLIS. I know I wouldn't. Would you?

MARTIN. Well, I haven't really grown up, yet.

PHYLLIS. (*Smiling.*) I don't believe you have.

TWO MEN

LABURNUM GROVE[1]

by

J. B. PRIESTLEY

GEORGE RADFERN *is to all who know him in Laburnum Grove, a respectable, middle-aged business man. However, through circumstances he has become a member of a large counterfeiting circle. He is self-assured under his quiet, affable manner.* INSPECTOR STACK *comes to see him. He is about forty. There is an air of authority about him.*

RADFERN *enters followed by* STACK.

RADFERN. Take a seat, Inspector.

STACK. Thanks. . . .

(*They both sit down, preferably near the table.*)

RADFERN. This is very interesting. I've never had the pleasure of talking to anybody from Scotland Yard before.

STACK. No, I don't suppose you have, Mr. Radfern.

RADFERN. Must have a very exciting life, you chaps. Different from some of us.

STACK. It's not as exciting as people seem to think. Most of it's dull routine, and very long hours at that. Not many quiet evenings at home.

RADFERN. Ah—that's a pity.

STACK. Yes, Mrs. Radfern was telling me this afternoon that you liked to be quiet at home, with your greenhouse and so forth.

RADFERN. Yes. My wife and daughter often laugh at me. They think I'm a very dull old stick.

STACK. Still, I've known wives and children go sadly wrong

---

[1] Copyright, 1933, by J. B. Priestley.

81

about men, and think they were leading one sort of life when all the time they were leading a very different sort of life.

RADFERN. Is that so? I've never struck that myself.

STACK. (*Meaningly.*) Really? Are you sure?

RADFERN. Well, I can't recall a case at the moment.

STACK. (*Meaningly.*) You surprise me.

RADFERN. But if there's anything I can tell you, I'll be only too pleased, though I can't imagine why you've taken the trouble to come and see me.

STACK. Trouble's nothing to us, Mr. Radfern, if the case is big enough. . . . You see for the last four years, at least, there's been a gang—a very clever, well-organized gang—who've been engaged in counterfeiting bank notes and treasury notes.

RADFERN. No? I shouldn't have thought it could be done, these days.

STACK. This gang operates here in England and also abroad, chiefly from Amsterdam and Brussels. Some of the notes are printed there, some of them here. Here's one of their notes. Perhaps you'd like to see it. (*Brings out pocket book and produces pound note.*)

RADFERN. I would. (*He brings out handkerchief and takes up note by one corner with a bit of handkerchief between his fingers and the note.*)

STACK. You needn't handle it as carefully as all that, Mr. Radfern.

RADFERN. Well, I thought one couldn't be too careful.

STACK. (*Softly.*) If I wanted your fingerprints, you know, I could think of better ways of getting them.

RADFERN. (*Examining note, laughs.*) Never occurred to me. I always thought this fingerprint business chiefly belonged to these detective yarns. Well, y'know, if this is a fake, it would take me in. I'm no expert, of course, but I'm in the paper trade, you know.

STACK. (*Significantly.*) So I understand, Mr. Radfern.

RADFERN. I wouldn't have hesitated a minute giving any-body eight half-crowns for this chap. Isn't it marvelous what they can do. Never would have thought it!

STACK. Surprising, isn't it? Oh—they're a clever lot.

RADFERN. They must be.

STACK. Humph!

RADFERN. Humph!

STACK. They've been clever at getting the right sort of pa-per, and with their engraving and printing, and with the way they've distributed the slush.

RADFERN. Slush?

STACK. Slush. And the Treasury and the banks haven't given us a minute's peace about this case. But at last we're getting results.

RADFERN. Splendid!

STACK. Yes, hundreds of little details that haven't meant any-thing much for months are now beginning to look like something.

RADFERN. Just like a jigsaw puzzle, eh?

STACK. That's it. Of course there are still a few pieces miss-ing, but not many—not many. It's only a matter of time now.

RADFERN. That's good, isn't it? You must be feeling very pleased with yourselves, eh?

STACK. We'd feel better still if we could just mop it all up now.

RADFERN. (Sympathetically.) Of course you would.

STACK. You see—this is how it often works in these cases— I hope I'm not boring you, Mr. Radfern.

RADFERN. Not at all, Inspector. Very interesting.

STACK. It works like this. We come across a nice little nest of clues in—say—Birmingham—

RADFERN. Birmingham will do. I was there only today.

STACK. And among these clues is a name, just one of several names in a notebook. And that name may turn up some-where else—perhaps in Glasgow—perhaps in Amsterdam.

Well, the owner of that name is perhaps passing himself off as an ordinary respectable citizen and business man. And he thinks he's safe. Do you follow me?

RADFERN. (*Beaming, but with sardonic emphasis.*) Yes, I should think I do. Poor devil. I can see it all. This chap imagines he's safe. And of course he isn't because you've got a lot of evidence against him.

STACK. Yes, a lot of evidence.

RADFERN. (*As before, but with more emphasis.*) And of course it's solid evidence, cast-iron solid evidence that wouldn't make you look silly if you took such a quiet respectable chap into a police court.

STACK. (*Now taking up the challenge.*) No, that's not quite it, because in this instance, we haven't bothered to pile up the solid evidence yet. But we've got one or two interesting little bits. Would you like to hear them?

RADFERN. I would, Inspector.

STACK. Well—for example—we know that a member of this counterfeiting ring arrived in Glasgow from the continent on the twenty-third of last month and was met by one of his confederates here. And we're pretty sure we can prove that this quiet respectable citizen we're talking about was also there, in Glasgow, on the twenty-third of last month.

RADFERN. In Glasgow on the twenty-third of last month? You know, that reminds me of something. The twenty-third? (*He takes out pocket diary and consults it.*) Not that I was in Glasgow. As a matter of fact I was in—

STACK. (*Quickly, triumphantly, standing.*) Newcastle. And so was this man who came from the continent. Not in Glasgow at all. That was a little trap and you walked straight into it.

RADFERN. (*Very calmly.*) Did I? I'm afraid I don't quite follow you there, Inspector. Bit too sharp for me, I expect.

STACK. (*Grimly.*) I shouldn't be surprised.

RADFERN. But what I was going to say was that I remember the twenty-third of last month because the Bowling Club

here had an outing that day—up the river first and then
finished off at the Palladium—and I was with them. About
twenty of us, there were.

STACK. (*Disappointed.*) Humph!

RADFERN. (*Quietly, but forcibly.*) Now that's what I was
meaning, you know, Inspector. Isn't that what they call an
alibi? Well, you know, if I was that man and you were
silly enough to rush me into court, that's the sort of thing
—an alibi like that—which would make you all look very
foolish, I imagine. Mind you, I know nothing about it—
but I've read some of these detective tales.

STACK. (*Walks away, then suddenly swings round.*) If you
were that man we're talking about, do you know what I'd
say to you?

RADFERN. I can't imagine.

STACK. I'd say to you straight out, look here, we *know* you've
been in this, but as yet we can't prove it, though sooner or
later we'll be able to prove it. But as the case has dragged
on long enough and we want quick results, don't wait like
a fool until we can put you in the dock, where nobody's
going to have any mercy on you, but tell us all you know
now—help us to clean the whole thing up—and we won't
even *try* to prove anything against you.

RADFERN. Well, of course, I can't answer for this man—

STACK. (*Sardonically.*) Never mind. Make an effort and try.

RADFERN. I fancy the first thing he'd say is that you're bluffing.

STACK. And do you know what I'd reply to that, just to
show him we weren't bluffing? First, I'd simply give him
two addresses: 59, Pool Road, Glasgow. And, 17, Bellingham
Street, Newcastle.

RADFERN. (*Admiringly.*) Just two addresses, like that. Isn't
that interesting now?

STACK. (*Grimly.*) Oh—he'd find it interesting all right. Then
I'd give him two names. Peter Korderman and William
Frazerly.

RADFERN. (*Keeping it up.*) You know, Inspector, this is as good as any of the films and detective tales to me. Better. It's a treat. Go on.

STACK. All right. Seeing that I'm putting some of my cards on the table, I might as well put this one. (*He produces half a playing card, the Knave of Diamonds.*) What do you think of that?

RADFERN. (*Examining the card.*) Half a Jack of Diamonds. That's grand. But you're not going to tell me these chaps you're after use a thing like this?

STACK. (*Ironically.*) We've got an idea they do. Sort of visiting card, you know, Mr. Radfern. Quite romantic, isn't it?

RADFERN. (*Shaking his head.*) That's the trouble. It seems a bit too romantic to me.

STACK. What do you mean?

RADFERN. (*Apologetically.*) Well, of course, I don't know anything about these things—

STACK. (*Grimly.*) No, no. We know all about that.

RADFERN. But I'd say offhand that this torn card business looks like a bit of leg-pulling. Too much in the story-book style, you know. Sherlock Holmes. Edgar Wallace. I can imagine some chaps—you know, chaps who like a bit of fun—just planting something like this card on you, to keep you guessing and to amuse you. (*Gives the card back.*) And that Carl Korderman you mentioned—

STACK. Peter Korderman.

RADFERN. Peter Korderman, then. Well (*Shaking his head.*) he doesn't sound quite real to me, you know, Inspector. Perhaps that's another bit of leg-pulling.

(STACK *stares at him speculatively, grunts, then walks away.*)

STACK. (*Suddenly turning.*) Now listen, Radfern. Let's drop this nonsense and talk straight.

RADFERN. Go on.

STACK. (*Accusingly.*) You're in this counterfeiting game. I know very well you are, and you know I know. That's straight talking, isn't it?

RADFERN. I don't know whether it's straight or not, but it seems to be very offensive talking.

STACK. Well, here's some more. We want convictions, of course, but what we want even more than that is to break up the ring as soon as possible, because the Treasury and the banks are at us all the time. Tell us all you know *now*, put the game into our hands, and we'll forget about you. And you know what it means if we don't forget about you. There'll be none of this my-first-offense-and-I-didn't-know-any-better humbug for you if you do find yourself in court. You'll get as much as the judge can give you, and that's plenty. Now what do you say?

RADFERN. (*Impressively.*) This is what I say, Inspector Stack. My name is George Radfern, and I'm in the paper trade and can prove it. I live at Ferndale, Laburnum Grove, Shooters Green, where I'm well known as a decent respectable citizen and a householder. I've been swindled myself in my time, but if ever I've injured any man, woman or child in this country, then it's news to me. And you haven't enough evidence against me to take me to that door. And you know it.

STACK. Give me a bit more time, and I'll take you a lot further than that door.

THE WIND AND THE RAIN [1]

by

MERTON HODGE

CHARLES *has come to a university in Scotland to study medicine. He is "a boy of eighteen, fair, with charm, and perhaps a little old for his years."* PAUL DUHAMEL *is a Frenchman of twenty-nine years, who is taking a post-graduate course. He has a marked accent. "Pale and dark, he makes a rather*

[1] Copyright, 1933, by Merton Hodge.

pathetic attempt to appear excessively English, but he never succeeds in hiding the foreigner."

CHARLES. (*On a sudden thought.*) Oh, I want to send a telegram.

PAUL. You can telephone it from here.

CHARLES. Oh. Can you? It's only to let my mother know I got here all right.

PAUL. The telephone is there. We put pennies in the box. (*Indicates box on wall.*) It simplifies matters at the end of the term.

CHARLES. Oh. I see.

PAUL. Do you want to send it now?

CHARLES. No. There's no hurry. So long as she gets it to-night. I nearly sent it from the station, but I wanted to see where I was going to live first.

PAUL. I see. A little homesick? (*Smiles.*)

CHARLES. (*With a laugh.*) Give me time!

PAUL. You'll have plenty of that.

(*Both laugh.*)

CHARLES. (*Tentatively.*) You're . . . you're . . . not English, are you?

PAUL. (*Essaying a dialect.*) Eh, laad, I come from Lancashire! (CHARLES *is a little embarrassed.*) No, I am a Frenchman. But I have lived in England a long time . . . and here . . . in this beautiful romantic city.

CHARLES. Oh.

PAUL. My childhood was spent in Paris. Do you know it at all?

CHARLES. Oh, Lord, yes. I love it. I've been there quite a lot with my mother.

PAUL. (*Amused.*) With your mother?

CHARLES. (*Laughs.*) I suppose it does sound a bit funny, going to Paris with one's mother, but she's pretty good at Paris. We've been to a lot of places together. We quite like it.

PAUL. That's nice.

CHARLES. You've . . . been here some time?

PAUL. Nearly nine years . . . off and on.

CHARLES. Good Lord . . . have you?

PAUL. I qualified here.

CHARLES. Oh! (*Nods.*)

PAUL. I want to get my fellowship, but I doubt if I ever will. I find it . . . difficult . . . (*Laughs.*) . . . to concentrate on anything for very long.

CHARLES. Sounds bad. (*Laughs.*)

PAUL. It is. It is not so easy. They . . . (*Smiles.*) . . . know me too well here. . . . I am a foreigner . . . (*A little bitter.*)

CHARLES. How demned silly!

PAUL. When were you last in Paris?

CHARLES. About two months ago.

PAUL. I like it for a time. It's my home. I go back sometimes, for various family ceremonies. What part of London do you live in?

CHARLES. Sloane Street. Do you know it? (*A little eager.*) My mother has a business there. . . . Antique furniture. . . .

PAUL. Not Mabel Tritton?

CHARLES. (*Smiling.*) That's us.

PAUL. (*With pleasure.*) But I know your mother.

CHARLES. (*Pleasantly surprised.*) Do you?

PAUL. I have met her. We have mutual friends. She is . . . very charming.

CHARLES. Have you really? How extraordinary! At least, I suppose it isn't really. She's fairly well known. She is rather a darling.

PAUL. You will find it all a bit different up here.

CHARLES. I'm expecting to. I gave them rather a stir at home with these the other day. (*He indicates the box of bones.*)

PAUL. What is that?

CHARLES. Bones. (*Laughs.*) Anatomical bones. I have to have them, don't I? I started in early to create a medical atmosphere. . . . Mother tied them up, as she was terrified they'd come open in the train. These come from France. Cost a fiver. . . . A bit hot, wasn't it?

PAUL. Coals to Newcastle, my friend. Wait. Look in here. (*He opens cupboard door left, and displays an assortment of old bones.*)

CHARLES. (*Looks into cupboard.*) Oh I say! Could I have used those?

PAUL. Yes, but it is just as well to have your own. Yours are new and clean. This town is full of students trying to sell their old bones. Ha! it is a source of great revenue in difficult times.

CHARLES. (*Puts suitcase on table.*) I've got a lot of books, too. I'd better show you those. They're probably all wrong. (*Opens suitcase.*) I wrote up and got a list—I suppose I should have waited. They're full of the most grisly illustrations. (*Hands* PAUL *a book.*) I need that, don't I?

PAUL. Gray's *Anatomy*. That's all right. It is one of those books always bought . . . and which makes an impressive spectacle on your bookcase. . . .

CHARLES. I know. Frightfully impressive. I had it in the bedroom for a week before I left. The maids were very intrigued.

(PAUL *has idly glanced at a large photograph in a travelling frame that* CHARLES *has left lying amongst the books on table.*)

PAUL. That's a charming girl. (*Interested, and reads on photograph.*) "Jill." Your sister?

CHARLES. Haven't got one. . . . (*Laughs.*) We've sort of grown up together. Families always been friends . . . and all that, you know.

PAUL. (*Amused.*) I know.

CHARLES. (*A little embarrassed, and busying himself with suitcase.*) It's going to be pretty foul without her. Funny how you realise those things, all of a sudden. . . .

PAUL. Um.

CHARLES. She's got no mother, so rather relies on mine. She's staying with mother now. It's grand knowing she's there. . . .

PAUL. (*Looking at his watch.*) I must go upstairs and get my coat.

CHARLES. Right.

PAUL. I'm sorry I cannot stay and talk . . . but . . . you understand.

CHARLES. Yes, of course. I've got an awful lot of sorting out to do here.

PAUL. Don't forget your telegram.

CHARLES. I won't . . . and thanks so much. . . .

PAUL. There's always beer in the cupboard.

CHARLES. Oh, thanks.

PAUL. (*Smiles.*) Well, cheero. . . . Tomorrow night perhaps we can go somewhere.

CHARLES. I'd love to.

PAUL. (*At door, with a parting smile.*) So long.

CHARLES. Good-bye.

SMALL MIRACLE [1]

by

NORMAN KRASNA

While waiting for a train that is to take TONY MAKO, *a criminal, to the penitentiary, he and* JOE TAFT, *a detective to whom he is handcuffed, go to see a musical comedy. The scene is the lounge of the theatre during an act.* TAFT *is about forty, an intelligent man and very human.* TONY *is about twenty-eight. His face does not suggest the hardened gangster from the East Side and his Italian accent is not very noticeable.*

MAKO. . . . Just let's talk, what do you say? I haven't talked to anybody so long I'm full of gab.

JOE. All right.

[1] Copyright, 1934, 1935, by Norman Krasna.

MAKO. What about your kid?

JOE. What about her?

MAKO. What are you giving her for a present?

JOE. You mean for a graduation present? Well, my wife's made her a dress—a regular ladies' dress—like an evening gown—but on a small scale. And I'm buying her ladies' shoes with high heels—say, she'll be crazy about it.

MAKO. I don't know. That's no present for a kid—getting clothes. I used to get birthday presents like that. My mother used to starve herself and get me a couple of handkerchiefs or a shirt. I didn't like that. I remember once I wanted an electric train. Geez, I wanted that train. Do you know what I got that Christmas? A suit of woolen underwear! I was nuts about machinery. Maybe if my folks had enough dough to buy me things I wouldn't 've learned to pick pockets for 'em. (*He breaks off from this mush.*) No, a dress ain't no present.

JOE. A girl thinks a lot of clothes.

MAKO. (*Reaching into his pants pocket.*) Say, listen, I got about six hundred bucks here. You want to do me a favor?

JOE. Don't be crazy.

MAKO. Now what am I gonna blow this dough on? You take five hundred and get the kid something from me.

JOE. I don't need any money!

MAKO. (*Pushing it into his hand.*) Now listen, Taft. I'd rather your kid get this than some crook warden. Come on. I got no one to give it to. (*He continues pushing it in* JOE's *palm.*) You know I'm right. That's it.

JOE. Thanks. It's a lot of money, Tony. . . . (*He takes out his cigarette case and puts the bills in it.*)

MAKO. You keep money in a cigarette case?

JOE. I wouldn't want this to get lost. What should I buy with it?

MAKO. Yeah, let's see. (*He puts the rest of his money back in his pocket.*) What did I always want? She don't like machinery, huh?

JOE. (*Putting the case in his coat pocket, nearest Tony.*)
Well—she's a girl—

MAKO. You better put that in your other pocket. I'll lift it
on you.

JOE. (*Laughing.*) That's O.K. I trust you.

MAKO. I'll forget myself. I'm the best pick-pocket you've
ever seen. Now what can we get your kid? How about a
stack of dolls?

JOE. She's a little too old for that.

MAKO. All the dames I know ask for jewelry. You can't get
much for five hundred, but you can get something. Maybe a
—(*He pantomimes a necklace.*) with a couple of little diamonds.

JOE. Well—if you want me to—except she's only a kid—

MAKO. Say! I got it! You remember I was just telling you
about that electric train? If somebody had come up to me
and asked me if I wanted the Brooklyn Bridge or that train
I'd have taken the train. Well, she wants something like
that, too. We'll give it to her.

JOE. An electric train?

MAKO. (*Disgusted with him.*) No. She don't want a train.
She's a girl; she's got something else in her mind. You go
up to her and just say this: Baby, what do you want? Anything in the whole world, I'll get it for you. You'll see it
won't even be five hundred bucks.

JOE. That's a good idea. She'll be getting something she
wants.

MAKO. Even if it's something nutty, get it. Say, if anybody
had said that to me, I'd remember it all my life. (*Seriously.*)
Only don't get her nothing that'll make her sick, like cake
or a lot of bananas. One time I got murdered on a dozen
bananas.

JOE. This is very nice of you, Tony.

MAKO. Better not tell her who it's from.

JOE. I'll tell her it's from an uncle out west.

MAKO. (*He grins.*) Yeah, from Colorado.

JOE. If there's anything I can do for you, Tony—if there's something you want.

MAKO. No—you can't do anything. I'd like two things to happen. First, I'd like to get Anderson in a dark alley for a couple of minutes; and second, after that—I'd like to drop dead. (*He turns slowly to* JOE, *who has been looking at him.*) You couldn't fix that, could you? (*He laughs shortly, bitterly.* JOE *looks at him pathetically. There is loud laughter from upstairs.* MAKO *looks upward.*) Let's go upstairs.

THE FIRST LEGION [1]

by

EMMET LAVERY

REVEREND MARK AHERN *is a member of the House of St. Gregory. He is about forty; "vigorous and virile, the romantic intellectual of the Society." Before taking his vows, he studied law, which training is still apparent.* DR. PETER MORELL *is "an aggressive confident physician" about the same age as* MARK. *He is a heretic. Just now he is unnerved. The scene is* FATHER AHERN'S *confessional booth.*

Kneeling at right angles to the audience and separated from FATHER AHERN *by the usual confessional screen is* DR. MORELL.

MORELL. (*In a frantic whisper.*) Don't you recognize me, Mark? It's I—Peter.

AHERN. Of course I recognize you but we try not to identify people. It's easier for them that way. What can I do for you?

MORELL. I didn't come to make a confession exactly—not a confession as you look at it. I haven't been to the Sacraments in years.

AHERN. What is it you want, then?

MORELL. I want to talk to you. I've got to talk to somebody. But first I want you to promise me something. (*Somberly.*) I want you to regard everything I say in as sacred confidence as if I were making a real confession to you.

AHERN. I promise you that everything you choose to tell me I shall hold strictly under the seal of confession.

MORELL. You're going to hate me, Mark. I've done a frightful thing. . . . I've tinkered with something that's beyond me . . . it's run away with me. . . .

AHERN. Control yourself, Peter. Now what is it that is bothering you?

MORELL. (*Blurting it out.*) Don't you see, Mark? *José's cure isn't a miracle!*

AHERN. (*Aghast.*) I knew it. I felt I was right all along. (*Then like a lawyer on cross-examination.*) How could it happen? What brought it about?

MORELL. José had a dream, that's all. When he awoke, the ecstasy of it was still upon him. He forgot his emotional paralysis, the fever broke—and he walked. That's all there is to it.

AHERN. (*Grimly.*) No, Peter. That's not all. What's the rest of it? (*Then more kindly.*) How could you do such a thing? I know you're not one of us but it isn't like you.

MORELL. (*With fleeting bravado.*) I always wondered about faith healing. Well, here was the chance to test it. All I had to do was let José think a miracle had touched him—and he was certain to walk.

AHERN. But why, Peter? Why were you willing to make fools of us all?

MORELL. (*Bitterly.*) I've hated the Society of Jesus . . . oh, I don't mean you and the others here particularly, but just all of you put together . . . and it amused me to think how some of them might behave once the world came back to them with so many of the things they had given up.

AHERN. (*Pityingly.*) And what did we ever do to you?

MORELL. What do you do to any man who has fallen away

from the Church? Most of the time you annoy me . . . you make me feel as if you are all too good to be true.

AHERN. (*The relentless cross-examiner.*) The other doctors? How did you manage to deceive them?

MORELL. (*Mockingly.*) Did you ever hear doctors disagree on the diagnosis of an appendix? How expect all of them to be accurate in the presence of a *synthetic miracle?*

AHERN. (*Very much dazed.*) The "cures" continue—such as they are?

MORELL. (*Excitedly.*) Yes, but I forgot one thing. What about the people who are disappointed? (*Shrilly.*) I never counted on that. I only meant to mock the Society. I never intended to hurt anyone else.

AHERN. Didn't you realize you could not hurt us without hurting others too?

MORELL. (*Fighting for coherence.*) Oh God, Mark. I forgot what it would do to children . . . they believe so hard. . . . Jimmy Magee, my sister's boy . . . his mother brought him all the way from the Coast . . . and he believes that he's going to walk. And he isn't, Mark. He can't. He isn't like José. Jimmy had anterior poliomyelitis when he was five . . . how can I tell him he isn't going to walk?

AHERN. That must be part of your just punishment: to let this poor boy see the truth.

MORELL. (*Brokenly.*) I can't, Mark. He's so sure. God—what have I done? What can I do?

AHERN. (*Vigorously.*) What can you do? There's only one thing to do. You will take steps at once to stop all these pilgrimages, as quickly as possible.

MORELL. And throw people into a panic?

AHERN. (*Grimly.*) No more of a panic than that of some who have made their whole lives over because of your miracle. (*Impressively.*) The Church does not live on error. You must tell Father Rector and those in authority and let it taper off slowly. You have done a terrible thing, but thank God you have come forward in time to let me save my House—

MORELL. (*In outright revolt.*) I have done nothing of the sort! I have simply come to you for advice—and I asked it under the seal of confession. *Don't forget that.*

AHERN. (*Note of terror in his voice.*) NO. No. No, Peter. You don't mean that. You can't mean it.

MORELL. (*In terror also.*) You are not to tell one word of what I said here. I had to talk, to someone I could trust, or—

AHERN. (*Speaking no longer as priest to penitent but flaying him as man to man.*) Someone you could trust? Why didn't you take your trust to someone else?

MORELL. I thought you were the right one to come to. You never were for the miracle.

AHERN. (*Bitingly.*) That's just it. Here I am the one person who could save this House and you bind my hands. You couldn't condemn a man to such a purgatory, Morell: to stand by helplessly and watch priests of God sanctioning such a blasphemy. I beg you: let me tell Father Rector before it is too late.

MORELL. Never. Never. It would kill José and God knows what it would do to Jimmy.

AHERN. Have you the faintest conception of what you are doing to me? Once you put upon me the seal of confession, I begin a living death.

MORELL. I can't help it, Mark. I can't tell and I won't.

AHERN. (*His despair mounting.*) Must I know the real truth of this all my life and say nothing? See my friends do the wrong thing and be powerless to stop them? Is there no pity in your soul, Morell?

MORELL. I must have lost my soul long ago. I'm only a feather tossed on the wind.

AHERN. (*Stingingly.*) And a white feather at that. I beg you —I command you—not as a priest to a sinner, merely as one human being to another, let me speak the truth and save my Order.

MORELL. (*Piteously.*) All you think of is the Society. I'm thinking of kids like Jimmy who might never believe in anything again.

AHERN. (*Scathingly.*) And what do you leave me to believe in? I would rather you had plunged a knife through my heart. It would be far easier to die defending the seal of confession as martyrs have done than to live out this tragedy of error for the rest of my days. God help me, Morell—I can not even curse you, as I should.

MORELL. I'd pray, if I could, Mark, but I don't know what to pray for. . . .

AHERN. (*Dropping to his knees.*) Morell, if you ever prayed in your life, you pray with me now—pray not for what you want but pray to God for what He wants. You have certainly put everything up to Him now . . . nobody else can do anything. . . . (*Then in great simplicity.*) Oh God, in whom all things begin and end, let Thy light shine upon us. Grant this man the grace to see the truth and the courage to speak it. Spare, we pray, these unfortunate people who keep coming here looking for something we are powerless to give them. Don't let this mockery continue, I beg of You—Show us the way, Oh Lord, or we perish!

ON TO FORTUNE [1]

by

LAWRENCE LANGNER AND ARMINA MARSHALL

TALBOT SLOAN *is president of the "Sloan National Bank" in a small town out West. He is a likable man of about fifty years, although he is inclined to be pompous.* TRACY *is the teller at the bank. He is about the same age as* SLOAN, *smiling, polite and dignified. A large block of bonds are missing at the bank, and the auditors are expected. Apparently thinking only of his duty to the town and the stockholders, but actually for his own protection,* TALBOT *substitutes other*

[1] Copyright, 1934, by Lawrence Langner and Armina Marshall. Reprinted by permission of the authors.

bonds in their place, considering it a legal technicality. The scene is TALBOT'S *home.*

TRACY *enters.*

TRACY. Good evening, sir.

TALBOT. Good evening, Tracy. Come in. . . . What do you want to see me about, Tracy? . . .

TRACY. (*Evasively.*) You see, Mr. Sloan, I know what a fine man you are—what a pillar of the community you are—and I want you to know that I respect you—

TALBOT. (*Worried.*) Yes, yes—go on.

TRACY. And I want you to bear in mind my respect for you, when I bring up certain points which bear on this "pillar-of-the-community" feeling—as it were—which I have for you.

TALBOT. Well, what's this all about? Grimm? The default?

TRACY. Yes, Mr. Sloan, in a way, the default. I might even say, *the default.*

TALBOT. . . . What are you talking about?

TRACY. (*Charmingly.*) The default which was quickly covered by removing securities from one place in the vault, and placing them in another.

TALBOT. What do *you* know about it, Mr. Tracy?

TRACY. I know *all* about it, Mr. Sloan.

TALBOT. What!

TRACY. I'm probably under suspicion myself, on account of this theft, sir. So I did a little investigating on my own, and I think you know what I found, Mr. Sloan.

TALBOT. I see.

TRACY. (*With kindly warmth.*) So knowing how badly you'd feel and having only your interests at heart, now as always, I came right to you about it.

TALBOT. (*In the friendliest tones.*) You were quite right, Tracy. There's been some thief at work, and I'm going to find out who it is. But meanwhile, it's imperative that nobody should know about this. I can trust you, can't I?

TRACY. Absolutely, Mr. Sloan, absolutely! That's what I

wanted to say. I'm sorry about all this, sir. . . . I hope what I am going to say does not add to your further discomfiture, for I like you, Mr. Sloan, and Mrs. Sloan too, and respect you no end. But I have come to ask you, at this time, to make up a few little personal losses to me on our bank stock, which I bought at your suggestion.

TALBOT. What!

TRACY. A hundred shares which I bought at 350. They're now down to 75. Now, all I ask is your signature to this note, which buys them back at the price I paid you for them.

TALBOT. Well, I'll be . . .

TRACY. I'm sorry about this, sir. I know how you felt about this. I know you wanted us employees to own our own stock in the Bank, and have been very good about giving us all the time in the world to pay for it at 1929 prices, but I've been getting tired of paying in half my reduced salary for the past four years. I hope you don't mind, sir.

TALBOT. Tracy, for over twenty-five years I've been under the impression that you were honest to the bone.

TRACY. I can appreciate your disappointment, sir. For twenty-five years I've had the same impression about you, sir.

TALBOT. I don't see the slightest justification—unless you intend to take advantage of this situation.

TRACY. You're putting it rather crudely, sir. . . . Besides, Mr. Sloan, since you *are* the pillar of the community, as it were, it's up to you to make good your mistakes. I wouldn't think of asking any reparation for my losses in interest.

TALBOT. That's very generous of you. (*Takes the paper from* TRACY.) Of all the barefaced pieces of blackmail . . .

TRACY. That's an ugly word, Mr. Sloan—not at all the way I intended you to feel. I have a boy in college, as you know. Oh, yes, and my wife has asthma and has to go South for her health every winter.

TALBOT. (*Ironically, as he signs.*) Tracy, to think I've had you working for me all these years, and never realized your possibilities.

TRACY. It takes an emergency like this to bring them out, sir. . . . (*Blandly as* TALBOT *signs the note.*) If anyone would have said to me three years ago, "Tracy, you'll be doing this one of these days," I'd have said, "Never, 'honesty is the best policy,'" but everything's changed. Mortgages are no good. Bonds can't be redeemed in gold. Gold isn't money any more—and here I am, doing this, and as cool as a cucumber.

TALBOT. Here you are. (TALBOT *hands note to* TRACY.)

TRACY. Thank you, sir. I certainly appreciate this, sir. Good evening, sir. (TRACY *exits.*)

PAGE MISS GLORY [1]

by

JOSEPH SCHRANK AND PHILIP DUNNING

CLICK *is a high pressure promoter who is down on his luck. He is amusing, kind-hearted but not too scrupulous.* ED *is a photographer. He is much more conscientious than* CLICK. *He is in love with* GLADYS, *of whom they speak.*

ED. (*Comes forward.*) Putting over a fast workout on me, huh! (*Starts to desk.*) I thought we agreed last night that we'd start in today cold.

CLICK. Oh—I just tossed a couple. How do we stand, anyway?

ED. (*Consulting slip of paper on desk.*) You bagged 119 out of 416 tries and I got 210. You owe me 840 dollars on the week. I'll settle for a ham sandwich. (*Picks up phone.*)

CLICK. Oh no. (*Puts hat on floor.*) Not 'til I get a chance to recoup. You ready to start? (*Takes card from pocket—sits.*)

ED. Let me wake up, will you? (*In phone.*) Hello—what time is it? Five-thirty! I left a call for four o'clock. Think I want to sleep all day! (*Hangs up and looks at* CHICK *indignantly.*)

CLICK. (*Shaking his head.*) That's the second time they slipped up on your call.

ED. You've been practising for three hours!

CLICK. (*Trying to take his mind off it.*) The service here is getting terrible.

ED. (*Picks up his hat from the floor, right center.*) In *my* hat too! (*Wipes it with his sleeve—puts on table center.*)

CLICK. (*Persisting.*) So terrible—I think we ought to move.

ED. *Ought* to move! I think we'll *have* to move! We're in a fine position to complain about the service. A fine hole you've gotten us into.

CLICK. Ed, you're rapidly developing into a liability. It began in Atlantic City when we were managing the dog track. Always afraid to try anything new.

ED. That last new thing got us fired. And that brilliant stunt you thought up of how to get even with them gave *me* a sore back.

CLICK. (*Feet on sofa.*) That buried alive attraction would have given the auditorium plenty of opposition—if the police hadn't dug you up.

ED. You know—I'm beginning to think Gladys has the right idea about you. She thinks you're nuts.

CLICK. I question that theory. I also question whether Gladys is well enough equipped to emit such opinions.

ED. (*Lights cigarette.*) She's well enough equipped to hold down a steady job—ever since we got back here.

CLICK. (*Scornfully.*) Stenographer! You call that a job! She hardly earns enough for us to borrow. (*Picks up empty cigarette package, throws it away.*) There's a pal for you— smoking our last cigarette! (CLICK *breaks cigarette in half and puts the unlighted half in* ED's *mouth.*) You know my brain doesn't function until I've had a smoke. (*Puff.*)

ED. Mine doesn't function until I've had breakfast.

CLICK. (*Starts tossing cards into hat.*) I've heard tell that if you starve yourself long enough your stomach starts to shrink and you don't have to eat hardly anything at all. (*One of the cards drops on the floor near the hat.* CLICK

picks it up and tosses it into the hat from a very close range.)
Take Mahatma Gandhi—

ED. (*Exits into bedroom—leaving door open.*) You take him.
CLICK. (*Tossing cards.*) I wish I could. If I ever had a guy
like that to promote, we'd never be in this tough spot now.
(*Waxing enthusiastic.*) You know what I'd do—(*Thinking
it all out.*) I'd have him walk into the lobby of the Waldorf,
wearing his loin cloth and leading his goat—walk right up
to the desk and register—Mr. Gandhi and goat! What con-
tracts I'd get him! Makes me dizzy to think of! (*Tosses another card.*)

ED. (*Appearing in doorway, dressing, picks up hat, puts it on
table.*) It's that empty stomach of yours. Hey, use your own
hat. What are we going to do about getting something to
eat?

CLICK. Are you really hungry, Ed?

ED. Hungry! I'm emaciated—can't you see? (*Sits.*)

CLICK. (*Feels his arm.*) You've got fifteen pounds good
starving on you yet.

ED. Kidding aside, Click. Don't you think we ought to at
least move back to a cheap room?

CLICK. No. Then we'd have to pay. (*Rises, crosses right in
the manner of one giving fatherly advice. . . .*) Always remember this, my boy, as you go through life; when you're living on credit, make a good impression. Order the best of everything. (*Goes into bedroom to get tie.*)

ED. Yeah—order the best of everything and see what you
get. . . .

CLICK. There you go worrying again.

ED. Click, you're marvelous. You can be down to your last
nickel and walk into an automat as though you had a slot
reserve. (*Exits right.*)

CLICK. You don't know what's going to happen to us today—tomorrow—why three days in this town—(*Buzzer
sounds.*) That may be the buzz of destiny now. Keep coming.

TWO WOMEN

THE DISTAFF SIDE [1]

by

JOHN VAN DRUTEN

MRS. MILLWARD *is a charming and lovable lady of about fifty years. She is the kind of person in whom people confide. She is quiet and unperturbed by the petty annoyances of life. Her daughter,* ALEX, *is an aspiring young actress. She is unable to choose between* TOBY, *for whom she would have to give up her career to go to America, and* CHARLES, *who could help her on the London stage. The scene is in* MRS. MILLWARD'S *room.*

ALEX. Well, I'll say good-night too, Mother.

MRS. MILLWARD. Don't you want to stay and talk?

ALEX. Talk?

MRS. MILLWARD. About yourself. Hasn't Toby asked you to marry him?

ALEX. Yes.

MRS. MILLWARD. And you've refused him?

ALEX. Not yet.

MRS. MILLWARD. But you're going to?

ALEX. (*Flopping suddenly on to the couch.*) I don't know what to do.

MRS. MILLWARD. Wouldn't you like to talk about it? . . .

ALEX. Well, marriage means my whole life. I feel there's so much now I might be missing.

MRS. MILLWARD. Such as?

ALEX. A good time here . . . success, perhaps . . . my own life . . . my job.

MRS. MILLWARD. What is your life but *his* life, if you love him? Besides, your marriage is your job.

ALEX. Supposing it fails?

MRS. MILLWARD. (*Countering her.*) Supposing your job fails? (*Pause.*) Are you still flirting with the idea of Charles?

ALEX. A little. . . . I have been . . . for what he could give me. Toby knows that. He despises me for it.

MRS. MILLWARD. I think he's right to despise you for it. You don't love Charles. You begin to make me doubt if you even know what love means. Have you no capacity for caring for anything at all, except yourself?

ALEX. I do care for Toby.

MRS. MILLWARD. But not enough to make your life his life?

ALEX. I might as well say he doesn't love me enough to make his life mine. Why not?

MRS. MILLWARD. Because that's not the way things are. Because you're a woman.

ALEX. What's that got to do with it?

MRS. MILLWARD. Everything! Unless you're of the kind that lives impersonally like Theresa. And then I think you're unfulfilled. I think that's what being a woman means.

ALEX. To submerge yourself and everything you stand for, in a man? To give up everything to him?

MRS. MILLWARD. It isn't giving up—it's an exchange for something so much more enriching than anything you could have alone. It's not a sacrifice—it's a fulfilment.

ALEX. And if he dies, what then?

MRS. MILLWARD. (*Very quietly, after a pause.*) Then your life's over.

ALEX. (*With a quick impatient laugh of contemptuous protest.*) Oh, really!

MRS. MILLWARD. To all intents and purposes. (*Melting a little.*) Darling, I know what I'm talking about.

ALEX. Is *your* life over?

MRS. MILLWARD. The best of it. Father *was* my life. I couldn't have asked a better.

ALEX. (*Growing a little embarrassed and frightened.*) But

. . . but your life's full. You're interested in things. You read. You're fond of music. You like to travel. (*Then very tentatively.*) You've us . . . Roland and me.

MRS. MILLWARD. Do you need me, really? You're grown up. You're ambitious. I hope you'll marry . . . if not Toby, then someone else. Does Roland need me? He shouldn't any more. No. Life for me . . . I think for most women . . . means more than that. It means existing in someone else, *for* someone else.

ALEX. If you believe that, then you must believe in suttee.

MRS. MILLWARD. Oh, no, you can't do that. You have to live your life out.

ALEX. Why, if it's over?

MRS. MILLWARD. Because I think there's another kind of life that comes from inside you . . . after your own life's done.

ALEX. After your married life, you mean?

MRS. MILLWARD. After your own personal life. It comes from what you've made of it, almost like a reflection of it. Without it you wouldn't be complete. Can you understand that?

ALEX. Yes . . . if you've the capacity. Oh, Mother!

(ALEX *begins to cry, rises and crosses to* MRS. MILLWARD. MRS. MILLWARD *puts her arm round her, holding her.*)

THE JOYOUS SEASON [1]

by

PHILIP BARRY

CHRISTINA, *a nun, has come to visit her brothers and sisters whom she has not seen since she left home. She is gay, sympathetic and sensitive with "a face eternally youthful, lit from within—"* TERRY *is her younger sister. She is really a fine girl though just now she is rude and cynical. It is Christmas Eve and* CHRISTINA *wants them all to go to Midnight Mass.*

TERRY. I'm not going. I don't qualify. (*A silence.*) And I detest hypocrisy. So please excuse me. (*For a moment she meets* CHRISTINA'S *silent, searching gaze, then moves to the table where she takes a cigarette from a box, standing with her back to* CHRISTINA. *The silence continues,* CHRISTINA'S *eyes still upon her.* TERRY'S *shoulders come together. She turns suddenly, and demands.*) Well?—What if I am? (CHRISTINA *raises her brows questioningly.* TERRY *laughs shortly.*) Say it! "changed"! (CHRISTINA *says nothing. A moment. Then:*) Well, you looked as if you thought it.

CHRISTINA. Did I, Terry?

TERRY. Well, even if it's so, I don't see that there's much to be done about it, do you?

CHRISTINA. I don't know.

TERRY. *I* do.—So do you mind if I go up now?

CHRISTINA. I think I should mind very much.

TERRY. Sorry, but I must. I've had rather a hard day. (*She moves toward the doorway.*) Good night. (*Near the doorway she stops. Again her shoulders come together. She turns.*) Well, Reverend Mother?

(CHRISTINA *smiles faintly.*)

CHRISTINA. Well, Terry?

(TERRY *returns a few steps toward her.*)

TERRY. I suppose you find me quite a little changed. (CHRISTINA *nods. A moment.*) Yes—I suppose it's contact with the world that's done it. But you see, I believe in it. I don't believe in dodging.

CHRISTINA.—Dodging.

TERRY. Mother was ill. She'd been ill a long time. If you didn't care about having a home of your own, you should have stayed on to look after her.

(CHRISTINA *nods.*)

CHRISTINA.—A life, a career you might have respected more than the one I chose.

TERRY. I think I should have respected it a very great deal.

CHRISTINA. I could not have been a good companion so much longer. There was—constantly something drawing me away.—You see, one time the Lord sat down with me for a moment, then rose and left me to follow Him. However much I loved you all, there was nothing to do but gather up my life and go.

TERRY.—And that doesn't seem to you selfish.

CHRISTINA. Of course. But I assure you that when it happens there's nothing else to do. Why, life wouldn't be worth living! (*A moment.*) I should not have said that, because it never is not.

TERRY. You don't think so?

CHRISTINA. I am sure of it.

TERRY. Well, if I could save mine by moving from here to there, I should stay where I am.

(*A moment. Then:*)

CHRISTINA. And I had always thought that life would be so good to you.

TERRY. You—you were mistaken.

CHRISTINA. But that you should lose your faith in it—you, Terry, who were life itself!

TERRY. I guess it went with my faith in Francis.

CHRISTINA. That too?

(TERRY's *head sinks.*)

TERRY. Everything. (*And she raises it again, sharply.*) But I'm not asking anyone to be sorry for me, thanks!

CHRISTINA. Not you.

TERRY. I guess I expected too much of marriage.

CHRISTINA. It would be difficult to. It would be easier not to expect enough. That sometimes happens among *us,* and when it does, it's very sad.

TERRY. Well, anyhow, I don't believe my husband loves me —how's that, for instance?

CHRISTINA. It is sad.

TERRY. And maybe I don't love him anymore—how's that?

CHRISTINA. That is sadder.

TERRY. Oh, not so, maybe. *He's* not the man I married—he's nothing like him. Why should I care? (*There is a moment's pause, then she continues:*) I don't know what it is, but the air's full of something.—Maybe there's someone else for him—I don't know. All I know is that there's something awful hanging over us. I do know that.—I feel it! *I* get some things out of the air myself—*my* thumbs prick too. (*Another moment. Then:*) I wish I could die. I *want* to die. (*She laughs brokenly.*) How's that, for instance? (*Then suddenly, blindly she reaches for* CHRISTINA's *hand, grasps it, bends her head over it.*) Oh, Christina—everything's so awful—

(CHRISTINA *strokes her bowed head.*)

CHRISTINA. I know—I know, dear.—We'll find something to do.

TERRY. Oh yes, we must! We must, or I'll go crazy! (*She presses her face hard against* CHRISTINA's *hand, and sobs.*) —Crazy.—I hate living— Why can't I die?

CHRISTINA. What was your word?—"Dodging"? (*She shakes her head decisively.*) Not you. Not any Farley.

TERRY. I think all of us are, in one way or another. I thought you were the first to.

CHRISTINA.—Something will come to us, dear. (*She raises her up and kisses her on both cheeks.*) We must wait.

TERRY. Wait!—That's all I've been doing—

CHRISTINA. And still we must wait.

THE OLD MAID [1]

by

Zoë Akins

From the novel by Edith Wharton

This is DELIA's *wedding day. As she sits before her mirror she is very calm. She has wealth and social position, and she is ambitious.* CHARLOTTE *is her cousin. She is a quiet girl, ac-*

customed to her rôle of "poor relation." Nevertheless you can
feel her sincerity and strength of character. She is in love
with CLEM SPENDER, *of whom they speak. The year is 1833.*

CHARLOTTE. (. . . *entering.*) May I come in?

DELIA. Of course. . . .

CHARLOTTE. (*Crossing the room, to* DELIA; *importantly.*) I've
something for you.

DELIA. But how pretty you look! I never saw you look so
well. . . .

CHARLOTTE. (*Looks down at the dress gratefully.*) I don't
often have a dress that's been made especially for me. Thank
you for giving me this one.

DELIA. (*Carelessly.*) Thank mamma. She wanted you to be
dressed properly, of course. . . . You haven't anything blue
I could carry, have you?

CHARLOTTE. (*Drawing a short breath.*) It's odd you should
ask me that. (*Looking at a small box in her hand.*) This is
blue.

DELIA. What is it?

CHARLOTTE. A cameo. It's a present for you—from Clem
Spender.

DELIA. (*Abruptly; startled.*) From Clem! But— . . .

CHARLOTTE. He asked me to give it to you. He unwrapped it
to take out a note that was inside. That's how I saw it was
a cameo, and blue. Then he changed his mind again and
gave me the note to give you, too.

DELIA. But I thought Clem was in Italy!

CHARLOTTE. (*Simply, but with a hard note in her voice.*) He
came home today. Just in time for your wedding. He hadn't
heard you were going to marry someone else. He thought
you must be ill because you'd stopped writing.

(*As* DELIA *opens the note,* CHARLOTTE *turns to go, but* DELIA
stops her before she can open the door.)

DELIA. Wait—don't go!

(CHARLOTTE *turns from the door and stands waiting while*
DELIA *reads the note. Then* CHARLOTTE *speaks again, very*

simply, but with the same hard note in her voice, as if she were steeling herself against saying more.)

CHARLOTTE. They'll play the wedding march next.

DELIA. I know. (*Suddenly she covers her face with her hands and speaks impulsively.*) Oh Chatty, I'm afraid!

CHARLOTTE. Of what?

DELIA. Of Clem! Of what he may say or do. There'll be champagne, and if he should take a glass too much—. Watch him, Chatty, will you? Be—be kind to him.

CHARLOTTE. I don't see how anyone could ever be unkind to poor Clem.

DELIA. (*Bending her head, sharply.*) Don't—!

CHARLOTTE. (*Coldly, but with some surprise.*) I didn't know you cared that much.

DELIA. You knew I loved him.

CHARLOTTE. I knew you told him so.

DELIA. I must not cry.

CHARLOTTE. You won't cry if you keep saying to yourself, over and over: "I'm marrying a Ralston; I'm marrying a Ralston."

DELIA. (*Defiantly; herself again.*) Yes, I *am* marrying a Ralston; and I'm glad.

CHARLOTTE. (*Without sympathy.*) Everyone's glad you're doing so well. They always expected you to, and you have. But I don't envy you, Delia.

DELIA. I don't want you to envy me; but I don't want you to hold my marriage to Jim against me, either.

CHARLOTTE. (*Stubbornly.*) When Clem went to Italy to study painting, two years ago, you promised to wait for him.

DELIA. I did wait—but if Clem wanted a wife, he should have stayed here and gone into his uncle's bank, and earned something.

CHARLOTTE. If he'd wanted you for his wife, he should have, of course. Trying to be an artist isn't the sort of thing you had any patience with.

DELIA. But I was patient. He promised to come back, if he

failed, and go to work. And if he had, I'd have married him; even though papa disapproved. I swear that.

CHARLOTTE. It never occurred to you, I suppose, that an artist couldn't possibly know whether he was a failure or a success, at the end of a single year?

DELIA. I thought, and I still think, he should have known there was nothing in art, for him, by that time, and have come back and settled down. And he would have if he'd cared enough.

CHARLOTTE. He cared. You needn't think he didn't—

DELIA. You needn't think *I* didn't!

CHARLOTTE. (*With feeling.*) Then why couldn't you have waited?

DELIA. I tell you I did wait! Not one year, but almost two. It was almost two years after Clem went away before I told Jim I'd marry him instead.

CHARLOTTE. Couldn't you have had the kindness, at least, to write Clem that you were going to marry someone else?

DELIA. I intended to. I—I—tried to.

CHARLOTTE. But you were ashamed.

DELIA. No, I was not ashamed! I—(*Wavering a little.*) I'm fond of Jim. And it seemed hopeless to wait for Clem. (*Then frankly, unhappily.*) I couldn't bear to be an old maid, Chatty.

CHARLOTTE. (*With a strange look of exaltation.*) I shall be an old maid because the man I love doesn't love me. Not for any other reason.

DELIA. (*Frankly surprised; delicately; patronizingly.*) Oh, Chatty—my dear! I'm so sorry. I didn't know there was anyone.

CHARLOTTE. (*Proudly; turning away from* DELIA's *sudden glance.*) No one has ever known. But I would have waited for him all my life.

DELIA. You think so, but life doesn't stop; one gets lonely; one wants children, and a home of one's own.

CHARLOTTE. *I* could have waited. (*Then she turns and goes*

*to the door. There she pauses, listening. Then she turns back
to* DELIA.) It's the wedding march!

DELIA. (*With an effort.*) I'm ready. (*Breathlessly.*) Remember, watch Clem.

CHARLOTTE. I'll not forget.

DELIA. (*Looking at the cameo.*) "Something blue." (*She slips
it into the bosom of her dress, takes her bouquet, and moves
across the room towards the door* CHARLOTTE *is holding open.
There she pauses long enough to whisper, as she steadies herself by laying a hand on the other's arm*:) Oh Chatty—I'm
trembling! (*But almost instantly she recovers her poise, and
with her head lifted passes* CHARLOTTE, *disappearing into the
passage outside, to the strains of the music, as the curtain
falls.*)

THE CRADLE SONG [1]

by

GREGORIO AND MARIA MARTINEZ SIERRA

English version by John Garrett Underhill

TERESA *has been left, a foundling, on the steps of a convent.
She has brought much happiness to the nuns who have
brought her up. She is full of life, yet she has absorbed the
teachings of the Church. In this scene she is eighteen years
old. She is leaving the convent to be married.* SISTER JOANNA
OF THE CROSS *bids her farewell, knowing well the earthly joy
that will go out of her life after* TERESA *leaves.*

TERESA *and* SISTER JOANNA OF THE CROSS *remain behind,
picking up and arranging the papers, patterns and scraps that
have been left on the seats or about the floor. They say nothing but presently* TERESA *throws herself on her knees before
the Nun.*

[1] Taken from "The Cradle Song," by G. Martinez Sierra, translated by
John Garrett Underhill, published and copyrighted by E. P. Dutton & Co.
Inc., New York.

TERESA. Sister Joanna of the Cross!

SISTER JOANNA OF THE CROSS. What do you want, my child?

TERESA. Now that we are alone, bless me while there is no one here to see—no, not one—for you are my mother, more than all the rest!

SISTER JOANNA OF THE CROSS. Get up. (TERESA *gets up*.) Don't talk like that! We are all equal in God's house.

TERESA. But in my heart you are the first. You mustn't be angry at what I say. How can I help it? Is it my fault, though I have struggled against it all my life, that I have come to love you so?

SISTER JOANNA OF THE CROSS. Yes, you have struggled. You have been wilful—(*Then seeking at once to excuse her.*) But it was because you were strong and well. When a child is silent and keeps to herself in a corner, it is a sign that she is sick or thinking of some evil. But you—

TERESA. *Ay,* Mother! Where do you suppose that I came from?

SISTER JOANNA OF THE CROSS. From Heaven, my daughter, as all of us have come.

TERESA. Do you really think that we have all come from Heaven?

SISTER JOANNA OF THE CROSS. At least you have come from Heaven to me. You say that I am your mother more than the rest; I don't know—it may be. But I know that for years you have been all my happiness and joy.

TERESA. Mother!

SISTER JOANNA OF THE CROSS. I was so glad to hear you laugh and see you run about the cloisters! It was absurd, but I always felt—not now, for you are grown up now—but for years I always felt as if you must be I, myself, scampering and playing. For I was just your age now, a little more or less, when you came into the Convent. And it seemed to me as if I was a child again and had just begun to live. You were so little, so busy—yes, you were—but I was busy too, if you only knew, before I entered here, at home in our house in the village. I was always singing and dancing, although we were very poor. My mother went out every day to wash in the river or to do housework—she had so many children!—and I was always carrying one about in my arms. And when I entered here, as I could do, thanks to some good ladies, who collected the money for my dowry—God reward them for it—although I had a real vocation, I was sorrowful and homesick thinking of my little brothers and sisters! How I used to cry in the dark corners, and I never dared to say a word! Then the Mother told me that if my melancholy didn't leave me she would be obliged to send me home. And then you came and I forgot everything! That is why I say you came to me from Heaven. And I don't want you to think I am angry, or ashamed—or that it has ever given me a moment's pain to have loved you.

TERESA. Is that the reason that you scold me so?

SISTER JOANNA OF THE CROSS. When have I ever scolded you?

TERESA. Oh, so many times! But no matter. I always tell Antonio, Sister Joanna of the Cross is my mother. She is my mother, my real mother! So now he always calls you Mother whenever he speaks of you.

SISTER JOANNA OF THE CROSS. My daughter, will you be happy with him?

TERESA. Of course! I am sure I will. He is so good, he is so happy! He says he doesn't know where it is all his happiness comes from, because his father, who is dead now, was more mournful than a willow, and his mother, poor lady, whenever anything happened to her that was good, burst right out crying. How do you suppose it was she ever managed to have such a boy? It must be that sad mothers have happy children. . . .

SISTER JOANNA OF THE CROSS. How you do love to talk!

TERESA. Isn't it foolish, Mother? Don't I? Listen! When you were little didn't you ever want to be a boy? I did. I used to cry because I thought then that I could have been anything I wanted to be—this, that, I didn't care what it was—Captain-General, Archbishop, yes, Pope, even! Or something else. It used to make me mad to think that because I was a girl I couldn't even be an acolyte. But now, since—well, since I love Antonio, and he loves me, I don't care; it doesn't make any difference any more, because if I am poor and know nothing, he is wise and strong; and if I am foolish and of no account, he is, oh, of so much worth! And if I have to stay behind at home and hide myself in the corner, he can go out into the world and mount, oh, so high—wherever a man can go—and instead of making me envious, it makes me so happy! Ah, Sister Joanna of the Cross, when she truly loves a man how humble it makes a girl!

SISTER JOANNA OF THE CROSS. Do you really love him so?

TERESA. More than life itself! And that is all too little. Maybe it's a sin, but I can tell you. Do you believe that we will meet in Heaven the persons we have loved on earth? Because if I don't meet him there and I can't go on loving him always just the same as I do now, no, more than I do now—

SISTER JOANNA OF THE CROSS. (*Interrupting.*) Hush! Peace! You mustn't say such things. It is a sin.

TERESA. *Ay,* Sister Joanna of the Cross! How sweet it is to be in love!

SISTER JOANNA OF THE CROSS. But he—he—does he love you too, so much?

TERESA. Yes, he loves me. How much, I don't know; but it doesn't make any matter. What makes me happy is that I love him. You needn't think that sometimes—very seldom, though—I haven't been afraid that perhaps some day he might stop loving me. It used to make me sad. But if I had ever thought that some day I could stop loving him— No, it would be better to die first; for then, what would be the good of life?

SISTER JOANNA OF THE CROSS. Ah, my child! To continue in God's love!

TERESA. Do you know how I would like to spend my life? All of it? Sitting on the ground at his feet, looking up into his eyes, just listening to him talk. You don't know how he can talk. He knows everything—everything that there is to know in the world, and he tells you such things! The things that you always have known yourself, in your heart, and you couldn't find out how to say them. Even when he doesn't say anything, if he should be speaking some language which you didn't understand, it is wonderful—his voice—I don't know how to explain it, but it is his voice—a voice that seems as if it had been talking to you ever since the day you were born! You don't hear it only with your ears, but with your whole body. It's like the air which you see and breathe and taste, and which smells so sweetly in the garden beneath the tree of paradise. Ah, Mother! The first day that he said to me "Teresa"—you see what a simple thing it was, my name, Teresa—why, it seemed to me as if nobody ever had called me by my name before, as if I never had heard it, and when he went away, I ran up and down the street saying to myself "Teresa, Teresa, Teresa!" under my breath, without knowing what I was doing, as if I walked on air!

SISTER JOANNA OF THE CROSS. You frighten me, my child.

TERESA. Do I? Why?

SISTER JOANNA OF THE CROSS. Because you love him so. For earthly love—I mean—it seems to me it is like a flower, that we find by the side of the road—a little brightness that God grants us to help us pass through life, for we are weak and frail; a drop of honey spread upon our bread each day, which we should receive gladly, but with trembling, and keeping our hearts whole, daughter, for it will surely pass away.

TERESA. It cannot pass away!

SISTER JOANNA OF THE CROSS. It may; and then what will be left to your soul, if you have set your all on this delight, and it has passed away?

TERESA. (*Humbly.*) You mustn't be angry with me, Mother. No! Look at me! It isn't wrong, I know. Loving him, I— he is so good, he is so good—and good, it cannot pass away!

SISTER JOANNA OF THE CROSS. But does he fear God?

TERESA. One day he said to me: "I love you because you know how to pray." Don't you see? And another time: "I feel a devotion toward you as toward some holy thing." He! Devotion! To me! And whenever I think of that, it seems to me as if I was just growing better, as if all at once I was capable of everything there was to do or suffer in the world —so as to have him always feel that way!

SISTER JOANNA OF THE CROSS. I hear someone in the parlor. Draw the curtains.

THE HOUSE OF CONNELLY [1]

by

PAUL GREEN

The CONNELLYS, *once wealthy landowners of the old South, are rapidly falling into decay. "The two surviving daughters of Connelly Hall, now late middle-aged spinsters, are laying supper in this dining-room, fetching dishes of food from the kitchen at the left.* GERALDINE *is tall and somewhat prim, with pallid aristocratic features;* EVELYN *is a few years younger and less austere."*

GERALDINE. I heard a gun shoot twice. And I looked out and saw her and Will standing together there in the fields.

EVELYN. Pshaw, Deenie, there's no harm in that, is there?

GERALDINE. (*Tapping the knuckles of one hand against the palm of the other, a habit she has when she is worried or undecided about something.*) I thought I'd speak of it to you, that's all.

EVELYN. Oh, he was talking to her about the farm. Uncle Bob says there never was such a person for farming.

GERALDINE. We don't know what sort of woman she is— . . .

EVELYN. (*Bending over and smelling the ham.*) Oh, isn't that heavenly? Well, anyway, she's about as pretty a poor-white girl as I ever saw. . . . (*Examining the ham.*) It browned splendidly, didn't it? (*With a low half-hearted laugh.*) Now Uncle Bob will be sick at his stomach again. (*Picking up the leather-headed gong stick.*) Shall I ring now?

GERALDINE. (*Standing back and appraising the table.*) Our Christmas supper is ready at last. Yes, ring.

(EVELYN *turns to the sideboard and strikes the gong with slow measured strokes. The two women grow still in their tracks listening as the soft musical tones go echoing through the house.*)

EVELYN. I never get tired of listening to it.

GERALDINE. (*Softly.*) Yes, it's beautiful.

EVELYN. Something so lonely beautiful in it. (*Half musing.*) For a hundred years it has called our people into this dining-room. (*Softly also.*) A hundred years.

GERALDINE. (*Turning with quick nervousness towards the door at the left.*) I was forgetting the coffee. (*She goes into the kitchen, and* EVELYN *moves over to the hearth and leans her head against the mantel. After a moment* GERALDINE *returns with the coffee pot, which she places on the table.*)

EVELYN. (*Staring at the fire.*) Through all the rooms it goes calling. (*Echoing the gong with sentimental and heartaching mournfulness.*) Nobody. Nobody.

GERALDINE. Of course there's somebody.

EVELYN. (*With sudden and tearful melancholy.*) How warm this fire is. It burned just like this Christmas years ago. I was standing here and Father came in from town. He'd brought me a new fur coat— You remember that coat, Deenie?

GERALDINE. Let's think of tonight, not some other night. Now that's it.

EVELYN. Oh, there was so much fun then. We had so many friends.

GERALDINE. (*With a touch of sharpness.*) We have friends now, Evelyn.

EVELYN. Yes, Mother, and Will, and Uncle Bob, and you and me. There were so many more then. Father—Grandfather —Aunt Charlotte and Uncle Henry. Soon there'll be Uncle

Bob and Will and you and me; then you and me and Will; then—

GERALDINE. *(Gazing about the room as if willing herself into the attitude of an interior decorator.)* These ivy leaves look better in the center of the table. *(She moves them from the side-board.)*

EVELYN. *(Gazing about the room also.)* It looks beautiful, Deenie—beautiful and sad.

GERALDINE. *(Aloofly and as if conscious that the portraits heard.)* This room is always beautiful—and happy to me.

EVELYN. *(Lighting the candles.)* Sad like a funeral. *(Childishly.)* Why don't you ever say so? You know it is.

GERALDINE. Set out the wine please, Evelyn. Mother says we must have some tonight.

EVELYN. *(Going to the window at the rear and looking out.)* It's getting dark and you can't see anything down in the garden there. *(With her face against the pane.)* Remember the Christmas we had that orchestra from Richmond? You danced with a naval officer that night—hours.

GERALDINE. *(With a little laugh.)* You remember a lot.

EVELYN. Sometimes I do.

GERALDINE. Come away from the window, silly, you'll catch cold.

EVELYN. *(Turning impulsively towards her.)* Deenie!

GERALDINE. Go see if Uncle Bob is ready.

EVELYN. Yes, I will. *(Dabbing her eyes with her handkerchief, she goes out at the right. GERALDINE stands lost in thought.)*

BURLESQUE [1]

by

GEORGE MANKER WATTERS AND ARTHUR HOPKINS

MAZIE *and* GUSSIE *are members of a mid-western burlesque show. They are rough in speech and manner and they have*

[1] Copyright, 1926, by George Manker Watters; 1935, by Samuel French.

had to work to get where they are. The scene is BONNY'S *dressing room, where they are waiting for their cues.*

MAZIE *enters, helps herself to one of* BONNY'S *cigarettes, lights it, picks up a copy of* Variety, *sits down left, smokes and reads.*
GUSSIE, *a beef-trust girl, wife of* BOZO, *the second comedian enters, proceeds to help herself to* BONNY'S *make-up. As she does so—says—*

GUSSIE. You better douse that cigarette. This fireman here is a tough bird.

MAZIE. I been dodgin' firemen all me life and they ain't one caught me yet.

GUSSIE. Well, if this one gets you it'll cost you ten smackers.

MAZIE. They'll have a fine time gettin' ten smackers out o' me and this my first week with the show.

GUSSIE. It's none o' my business. I'm just warnin' you, but it's none of my business.

MAZIE. You took the words out o' me mouth, dearie. As long as you know I'm none o' your business we'll get along great.

GUSSIE. How do you like this show?

MAZIE. The show's O.K. but I ain't goin' to waste no love and kisses on some o' the people.

GUSSIE. Say it ain't so, dearie, say it ain't so. (*Is now vigorously powdering her ample bosom again.*)

MAZIE. Why don't you use the whole can. . . . Say what are all the dames weepin' over Sylvia Marco for?

GUSSIE. She's leavin' for New York tonight, to go in the Manhattan Follies.

MAZIE. Yeah, I know, but why the cryin'?

GUSSIE. Chorus girls don't have to have no reason for a good cry. (*Pause.*) Maybe they're cryin' 'cause they're glad.

MAZIE. Well, I almost feel like cryin' myself for I was hopin' to take one good punch at that dame. (*Eyeing* GUSSIE.) But maybe there'll be others.

GUSSIE. Bonny don't like her too—never speaks to her. I wonder why.

MAZIE. If Bonny don't like her there's a darn good reason. Bonny's the best scout in this game.

GUSSIE. You said it. Bonny's a good kid, but she does mix up with some awful fish.

MAZIE. (*Taking in* GUSSIE.) Yeah, so I've noticed.

GUSSIE. Some of 'em wise fish. Wise soubrettes.

MAZIE. Say, you know I'm plannin' to stay with this troupe a while and they ain't no special hurry about stagin' a battle, but I don't exactly take to that last crack o' yours.

GUSSIE. No? Well, what are you goin' to do about it?

MAZIE. (*Rising.*) I'm just goin' to take one sock at you to see how soft you really are.

GUSSIE. (*Taking a step toward her.*) All right Polly Pushover. Come on.

THE TRUTH GAME [1]

by

IVOR NOVELLO

ROSINE *is a wealthy, young society widow, who loves her money for what it can give her. She is both envied and adored by her friends.* EVELYN *is a very voluble person, rather insincere, and at all times the business woman. The scene is* ROSINE'S *house in Mayfair.*

ROSINE. (*From inside door up right.*) Hello, Evelyn.

EVELYN. Hullo, darling—(*Moving down to settee.*)—I was passing, and couldn't resist popping in for a moment. Darling, how enchanting you've made this room. . . .

ROSINE. (*Inside.*) What?

EVELYN. I said "how enchanting."

ROSINE. Can't hear. I'm coming out to make you a cocktail. (EVELYN *opening her handbag and looking at herself in the*

[1] Copyright, 1929, by Samuel French, Ltd.

mirror. Enter ROSINE *in a lovely dressing-gown.* EVELYN *rising and coming to the corner of table to center. They embrace.*)

EVELYN. My sweet! Oh, I see you took my advice. (*Walking round her—pointing to dressing-gown.*) She is marvellous, isn't she? and so cheap.

ROSINE. Well, do you know, I don't think so.

EVELYN. How much?

ROSINE. Fifty guineas. Of course, it's got a little coat and it was a model.

EVELYN. You're sure it was fifty?

ROSINE. (*Behind table, mixing cocktails.*) Quite—sent her a cheque this morning.

EVELYN. (*Rather annoyed.*) She told me twenty-five—what brutes they all are—trying to do me out of half my commission. Have you bought much else there?

ROSINE. Three evening dresses, a cloak, too lovely—some country clothes—

EVELYN. (*Sitting in armchair right center.*) How much in all?

ROSINE. Exactly two hundred and fifty.

EVELYN. But my dear, that's too divine—at ten per cent., that's twenty-five to me—you really are an angel.

ROSINE. Cocktail?

EVELYN. Thanks, dear!

ROSINE. (*Pours out cocktail, gives it to* EVELYN.) Forgive the horrible glasses,—Harris had an accident with an entire tray of Venetian ones.

EVELYN. (*About to sip her cocktail.*) My dear, I know of a shop where you can get the most exquisite glass—the sort with—

ROSINE. (*Pours cocktail for herself.*) So do I—I'm going there tomorrow—they've just opened—it's a branch of Salviati's from Venice.

EVELYN. (*Rising, very interested.*) Salviati's? I don't know about them. (*Sitting right of table left center, all smiles.*) Who sent you?

ROSINE. (*Standing behind table.*) No one.

EVELYN. Where are they?

ROSINE. Davies Street. (*Moving away round back of settee to left of same.*)

EVELYN. I think you might go to my little shop.

ROSINE. (*Smiling.*) Ten per cent.?

EVELYN. (*Sitting on chair right of table.*) Of course.

ROSINE. You are marvellous, Evelyn. (*Putting her feet up on settee.*)

EVELYN. I have to be—four hundred a year doesn't go very far.

ROSINE. How much do you make?

EVELYN. Commissions—(*Considering as she looks at cocktail.*)—about four thousand.

ROSINE. (*Rather astonished.*) Four thousand?

EVELYN. Something like that—after all, what's the point of knowing rich people without getting anything out of it? (*Finishes her cocktail, putting glass on table.*)—I used to have such a dreary time—twelve-thirty, the Ritz, on the chance of finding someone waiting for someone who was late—one could count on a cocktail—even if lunch didn't materialize (*Leaning back in her chair contentedly.*)—the Berkeley was splendid, they've so many entrances. One can go in and out six times without meeting the same people—since I've started my ten per cent. *I* give the lunches—and I get ten per cent. off *them*. I sold two motor-cars last week.

ROSINE. Is that why I always see you in a different one?

EVELYN. Yes, it's most awkward sometimes. I go to lunch in a yellow car—I come out, and it's bright blue. Life's agony—thank Heaven for the week-ends—except this one may be the last.

ROSINE. The last?

EVELYN. In that particular house—I think I've sold it.

ROSINE. But you've only had it a month.

EVELYN. I know, isn't it sickening—such a pretty house too. I wish it were mine, but there—it means two thousand commission if I sell it—the biggest thing I've ever pulled off—

and I don't mind telling you I need it—my overdraft is strained to breaking-point; my bank manager—such an attractive man—has taken to writing me insulting letters.

ROSINE. (*With a little laugh.*) Well, I hope you do sell it.

EVELYN. Thank you, darling, you are so sympathetic. You'll come down early on Saturday, won't you?

ROSINE. (*Just on the point of agreeing.*) Who else is coming?

EVELYN. Sir Joshua Grimshaw.

ROSINE. (*Looking rather horrified.*) Why?

EVELYN. He's the man that's got to buy the house: that's why he's asked.

ROSINE. Does he know he's got to buy the house?

EVELYN. (*Shaking her head slyly.*) Not yet, but he will.

ROSINE. Who else?

EVELYN. Joan Culver—poor darling—I felt I had to ask her —she's been out far too long—I keep telling her she ought to write a book of reminiscences.

ROSINE. What about?

EVELYN. How to be an *ingénue* through three reigns.

ROSINE. (*Laughing.*) Anyone else?

EVELYN. Vera Crombie.

ROSINE. Why—are you having the house done—decorated?

EVELYN. No, but Vera's very good at suggestions. You've got to watch her though.

ROSINE. How?

EVELYN. I asked her over to tea one Sunday—she was staying quite near—and quite casually I asked her what could be done with the drawing-room, and she gave the room one sour look and said, "Nothing, darling."

ROSINE. Helpful.

EVELYN. The next day she sent me a bill for five guineas for professional advice.

ROSINE. What ever did you do?

EVELYN. Sent her a bill for the tea she'd eaten—no money changed hands. . . .

ROSINE. (*Rising and turning up on left of settee.*) Darling, I must fly and dress—but don't go. Perhaps I can drop you.

EVELYN. That'll be too divine. (*Rises.*)

ROSINE. Give yourself another cocktail.

(*Exit* ROSINE *up left, partly closing the door.* EVELYN *tiptoes to door left, closes it, goes to telephone, looks up a number in the book.*)

EVELYN. Regent double-oh-oh-one double-oh-oh-one— Hullo! Is that Salviati's? Mrs. Brandon speaking. I should like to speak to the manager—all right. Hullo! This is Mrs. Brandon speaking. I hear you've only just opened? I'm so glad. I'm going to send you lots of people—not at all, I want you to be a success—a great success—I shall expect a handsome commission. Please don't laugh. If I make up my mind to make a shop—it's made. People are only too delighted to give me a commission—sometimes as much as fifty per cent. —Ten? Very well, but I usually get fifteen. I'm sending in a Mrs. Browne of Curzon Street—tomorrow, I believe, so don't forget—she's my customer. I'll write you tonight confirming the arrangement. Good-bye. (*Puts receiver down and moves up and looks outside door right and fans herself.*)

GROUP SCENES

MEN IN WHITE [1]

by

SIDNEY KINGSLEY

The scene is the doctor's library in a large, city hospital.
GEORGE FERGUSON *just finishing his interneship and about to
be married "is about twenty-eight; . . . slightly stooped from
bending over books and patients; a fine sensitive face, a bit
tightened by strain, eager eyes, an engaging earnestness and
a ready boyish grin."*

FERGUSON *looks for a particular book in the shelves.*

MICHAELSON. (*Another interne.*) Say, there's a damned in-
teresting article on Hochberg in this week's A.M.A.
FERGUSON. I know. (*He finds the magazine and hands it over
to* SHORTY, *a small, chubby, good-natured, irresponsible, wise-
cracking fellow, who takes life in his stride.*) Here it is. You
want to read this, Shorty.
(SHORTY *sits down to read it.*)
MICHAELSON. Yep. I wish I could get in with him for a
year. . . .
FERGUSON. (*To* SHORTY.) What do you think of that first case?
The way he handled it? Beautiful job, isn't it? Beautiful!
PETE. (*Interne, a tall, gawky lad, slow moving and casual
about everything but food, enters, fixing his stethoscope. He
drawls.*) Say, George . . .
SHORTY. Pete! Sweetheart! You're just the man I've been
looking for.
PETE. (*Drily.*) The answer is no.

SHORTY. Will you lend me your white tux vest for tonight? I've got . . .

PETE. (*Abruptly.*) The answer is still no. (*He turns to* FERGUSON.) That little—

SHORTY. (*Sits down again.*) Thanks!

PETE. You're welcome. (*To* FERGUSON *again.*) The little girl we just operated on is coming out of her ether nicely. I was kind of worried about the preop Insulin.

FERGUSON. Why? How much did you give her?

PETE. Forty units.

FERGUSON. Twenty would have been enough.

PETE. I know.

FERGUSON. Then why the hell did you give her forty? You might have hurt the kid.

PETE. Dr. Cunningham ordered it.

SHORTY. That dope—Cunningham!

FERGUSON. You should have told me before you gave it to her. I'm not going to have any patients go into shock on the operating table! Understand?

PETE. O.K.

FERGUSON. (*Good-naturedly, slapping* PETE *on the head with a pamphlet.*) If this happens again, Pete, you get your . . .

PETE. O.K. . . . Say, I'm hungry! Somebody got something to eat?

SHORTY. What, again? (PETE *looks at him with scorn.*) Lend me your white vest for tonight, will you, Pete? I'll fix up a date for you with that red-head.

(*Phone rings.*)

PETE. (*Nodding at* FERGUSON.) Fix him up.

(FERGUSON *laughs.*)

SHORTY. It'd do him good. That's the trouble with love— . . . (*Indicates the phone.*) Pete! Phone!

PETE. I was once in love myself. (*He starts for phone.*) But when it began to interfere with my appetite . . . No woman's worth that! (*They laugh.*)

FERGUSON. Thing I like about you, Pete, is your romantic nature.

PETE. (*On phone.*) Dr. Bradley! O.K. I'll be right up! (*He hangs up.*) Yep. At heart I'm just a dreamer.

SHORTY. At heart you're just a stinker!

PETE. Thanks!

SHORTY. (*Quickly.*) You're welcome.

(PETE *goes toward the door.*)

FERGUSON. Going upstairs, Pete?

PETE. Yep.

FERGUSON. (*Gives him bottle of sputum.*) Will you take this to the path lab? Ask Finn to examine it and draw up a report.

PETE. O.K. . . .

FERGUSON. Tell him to give it special attention! It's a friend of Hochberg's.

SHORTY. (*Follows* PETE *to door.*) I take back what I said, Pete. You're a great guy, and I like you. Now, if you'll only lend me that white vest. . . .

PETE. No!

SHORTY. Stinker! (*They exit.*)

NINE PINE STREET [1]

by

JOHN COLTON AND CARLTON MILES

MRS. HOLDEN *"is a pleasant, smiling, fragile woman" living in New England in 1886. Her daughter,* CLARA, *is a pretty quiet girl.* ANNE, *general houseworker, has been with the* HOLDENS *a long time, and speaks as though one of them.*

MRS. HOLDEN. (*Crosses to table right center.*) I do believe my luck held out again. I've stuck a straw in it and it's light as a feather.

CLARA. Oh, it's beautiful, Mother.

ANNIE. Much too good for some Presbyterian mouth to water on. (*Exits left.*)

MRS. HOLDEN. I do hope everything will go all right today. Anyway, there's no danger of rain.

CLARA. (*Gets cake box from chest and places it on table.*) Mother, Effie's always wondering why you work so hard trying to make things successful for the church.

MRS. HOLDEN. I don't. I guess I was just brought up that way. I've never known the time when everybody didn't have to work just as hard as they could work to make things right when there's more than four people concerned in 'em.

CLARA. (*Gets tissue paper from chest.*) Effie says that people have to work harder for a church than for a woodpile— Oh, Mother—! (*As she speaks,* MRS. HOLDEN *gives a slight gasp and the cake slides onto the table when she half falls into chair left of table.*) Mother— (*Calls.*) Annie, get some water—quick— (*To* MRS. HOLDEN.) You've worked too hard! Oh, why did you work this way?

(CLARA *fans her and* ANNIE *returns at once with dipper of water.* MRS. HOLDEN *gives slight gasp and comes to herself.*)

ANNIE. Killin' herself on church work. I come from church workers myself but I don't kill myself for nobody.

MRS. HOLDEN. I'm all right.

CLARA. Mother, you shouldn't overdo this way. You know what Doctor Powell said.

MRS. HOLDEN. I'm all right.

ANNIE. Better lay down, Mrs. Holden.

MRS. HOLDEN. No—it was awfully hot in the kitchen.

ANNIE. I'll go get your digitalis. (*Crosses right below table.*)

MRS. HOLDEN. No—no— (ANNIE *returns and takes dipper.*) I don't need it. I'll be all right. Don't say anything to your father, Clara. He'll make me stay home. I want very much to go to the clambake—I want to hear Mr. Pitt speak. He's so eloquent.

ANNIE. Ain't Mr. Pitt coming here to go with you folks?

MRS. HOLDEN. He's asked Effie to drive to the picnic in his gig.

CLARA. Mother, do you think that Effie and Mr. Pitt—? (ANNIE *eases to left center.*)

MRS. HOLDEN. Goodness knows! I hope so.

ANNIE. But he's only an assistant pastor, but mark my words, that young man will have a church of his own soon.

MRS. HOLDEN. We're all sure of that.

ANNIE. I never knew Effie to take such an interest in anyone before. (*Exits left.*)

MRS. HOLDEN. It makes me very happy. I used to think when Effie came back from the seminary she wouldn't find anyone good enough for her here. (*Starts to rise.*)

CLARA. No, Mother—you stay just where you are. I can do all this myself. (*Forces her back in chair.*)

MRS. HOLDEN. Your Aunt Maria wrote me all about Mr. Pitt—his mother was Emily Jenks of Dorchester. I went to school with her. But when I was married and came here we lost track of each other—

CLARA. Yes, Mother, I know.

MRS. HOLDEN. If it's God's will for anything to happen between Effie and Emily Jenk's son, I'll be happy.

ANNIE. (*Enters left with jar of pickles.*) After Effie left school and went visitin' her Aunt Maria in Boston she learnt pretty stylish tricks. (*Places basket on chair left.*) She had nineteen handkerchiefs in the wash last week. Seems when people get stylish they get kinder careless about handkerchiefs and towels. Every time she uses a towel she throws it in the clothes basket. (*Exits left.*)

CLARA. Annie believes in each four corners of a towel.

MRS. HOLDEN. (*Rising.*) I guess it's pretty near time to go upstairs and change my dress. The surrey from the livery will be here soon. What'll I wear—the challie?

CLARA. (*Joins her and walks to stairs with her. Does not help her.*) I think the taffeta would be nicer, Mother. You know you're kind of representative.

MRS. HOLDEN. Effie says we should be as simple as could be today. She went to a picnic at Cape Cod and all the ladies wore gingham. And there were Cabots there and Thayers and Lodges. Is Effie dressing?

CLARA. She's down at the wharves with Uncle Jim to see *The Dauntless* sail.

ANNIE. (*Enters left and crosses to them.*) If I was you, Mrs. Holden, I'd go upstairs in a hurry. Mrs. Doctor Powell is just stepping across the path. You'll save yourself a lot of digitalis if you miss her.

MRS. HOLDEN. Annie, don't be so unneighborly. Still—

CLARA. Go on, Mother. We all understand Mrs. Powell.

MRS. HOLDEN. (*Starts upstairs.*) Annie, take out the scalloped oysters in just ten minutes. (*Climbs stairway.*)

NINE TILL SIX [1]

by

AIMÉE AND PHILIP STUART

MRS. PEMBROKE *is a middle-aged woman, proprietress of a millinery and dressmaking shop. She is interviewing* GRACIE ABBOT. GRACIE *has "an eager attractive personality. Sometimes she drops her h's and sometimes she doesn't, but her voice is pleasing."* MRS. ABBOT, *her mother, "is a neatly-dressed little woman who looks as if she had worked too hard all her life. She has an air of simple dignity."*

MRS. ABBOT *hesitates on the threshold.*

MRS. PEMBROKE. (*Smiling at her.*) Oh! come in and sit down. (*Pointing to the armchair left center.*)

MRS. ABBOT. Thank you kindly.

(MRS. ABBOT *comes down into the room, pauses uncertainly*

for a moment, then sits left center. GRACIE *remains standing on her right.*)

MRS. PEMBROKE. (*To* MRS. ABBOT.) I'm afraid I didn't quite catch your name?

MRS. ABBOT. Mrs. Abbot.

MRS. PEMBROKE. Well, Mrs. Abbot, I understand that you want your daughter to come to us?

MRS. ABBOT. I won't go as far as that, Mrs. Pembroke. If I'd my way, I'd sooner she stayed at 'ome.

GRACIE. Mother!

MRS. ABBOT. You see, she's the oldest of five. So there's plenty for 'er to do.

MRS. PEMBROKE. Yes. There must be.

GRACIE. Mother, you said you'd let me come if I got the chance.

MRS. ABBOT. So you can. (*To* MRS. PEMBROKE.) I just want to make sure that she's in the right hands.

MRS. PEMBROKE. Of course you . . . Well, Gracie, why do you want to come to business?

GRACIE. I want to see life. I don't want only to be at 'ome.

MRS. PEMBROKE. I see. And why did you choose dressmaking?

GRACIE. It's either that or bein' a typist! I don't want to sit typewriting all the rest of my life.

MRS. ABBOT. She never was a one for sittin' still.

MRS. PEMBROKE. Well, if you come here, you ought to go into the workrooms for a year or two. That means sitting.

GRACIE. Do I have to?

MRS. PEMBROKE. Only if you want to get on. Do you?

GRACIE. Sure—an' I do—

MRS. ABBOT. I daresay she'll be gettin' married.

GRACIE. No, I shan't. Gettin' married only means a lot of kids and no time to yourself the whole blessed day!

MRS. ABBOT. Gracie Abbot!

GRACIE. It's gettin' their breakfast and washin' up; then it's gettin' their dinner and washin' up; then it's gettin' their tea and washin' up—and then you haven't properly started in!

MRS. ABBOT. Don't you be listenin' to her, Mrs. Pembroke.

GRACIE. You don't know what it's like!

MRS. ABBOT. They're all like that nowadays. They none of them want to do anything that looks like bein' a bit dull.

MRS. PEMBROKE. Did young people ever want to do anything dull?

MRS. ABBOT. I 'ad to.

MRS. PEMBROKE. So had I. But I didn't want to.

GRACIE. (*Brightening.*) There! Me mother always tries to make out that *she* did. (*Sitting on the arm of her mother's chair.*)

MRS. ABBOT. Gracie! That's too bad! Get up!

GRACIE. (*Rising.*) So you do, mother. You always go on as if people that didn't want to drudge all the time had something the matter with them.

MRS. PEMBROKE. That's just our way, Gracie. We know drudgery's hateful. You're quite right to say so while you can.

MRS. ABBOT. If you'll excuse me, Mrs. Pembroke, I don't think you ought to be encouragin' 'er. She's quite bad enough as it is.

MRS. PEMBROKE. Well, I think a lot of harm can be done to young people if they get it into their heads they're doing wrong, when they're only being—well, just young.

MRS. ABBOT. I've been at it myself since I was fourteen, that's all I know about it.

MRS. PEMBROKE. And I've been at it since I was twelve.

MRS. ABBOT. Twelve? You don't mean to say you started work when you were twelve?

MRS. PEMBROKE. And in the workroom! Sitting sometimes till twelve o'clock at night.

MRS. ABBOT. That ought never to've been allowed.

MRS. PEMBROKE. Anything was allowed in those days. Well, Gracie, as you've made up your mind not to sit, what about running about to see how you like that?

GRACIE. How d'you mean, Mrs. Pembroke?

MRS. PEMBROKE. Our busy season is just starting. That means there's a lot of extra fetching and carrying to be done. Each saleswoman has her own juniors, but one of them is usually out at lunch or away with a cold. So your job would be to take the place of whoever happened not to be there.

GRACIE. Does that mean you're goin' to take me on?

MRS. PEMBROKE. It looks like it.

GRACIE. (*Turning delightedly to her mother.*) Mother, did you hear that?

MRS. PEMBROKE. Quietly, please!

GRACIE. (*Pulling herself up, her hand to her mouth as before.*) I'm ever so sorry—

MRS. PEMBROKE. You'll only be on trial, you know. It's up to you whether you stay.

GRACIE. I'll try hard enough, if that's any good.

MRS. PEMBROKE. It helps. The important thing is to do as you're told. The saleswoman may not always speak to you just as you like, but you'll have to put up with it.

MRS. ABBOT. It's more than she does when 'er father speaks to 'er.

MRS. PEMBROKE. You see, it's not an easy job selling to people who want to get out of the shop without buying anything.—The customer must never be made to feel she's being kept against her will, but she has to be kept.—If she doesn't buy from us she'll buy elsewhere. You understand?

GRACIE. Yes.

MRS. PEMBROKE. Then you must learn to know the stock, so that when anything is wanted you will be able to fetch it at once. Our model-girls, or mannequins as they're called, are not supposed to do anything except show off the clothes.

GRACIE. (*Her eyes glowing.*) That's what I'd like to do.

MRS. ABBOT. (*Sharply.*) Don't you let your father hear you say that!

MRS. PEMBROKE. Why not, Mrs. Abbot?

MRS. ABBOT. 'Er father's very particular—

MRS. PEMBROKE. So am I. My mannequins are very nice girls. They just happen to have the correct measurements, that's all.

MRS. ABBOT. She's got quite enough ideas as it is.

MRS. PEMBROKE. (*After a moment's pause.*) Now as to salary! You'll get fifteen shillings a week for the first three months; after that a pound and after that—well, it depends on yourself. Does that meet with your approval, Mrs. Abbot?

MRS. ABBOT. It sounds fair enough.

GRACIE. (*Eagerly.*) Could I start straight away?

MRS. PEMBROKE. Ask your mother.

GRACIE. Could I, Mother?

MRS. ABBOT. It's all one to me. (*Resigned.*)

GRACIE. (*To* MRS. PEMBROKE.) I can!

MRS. PEMBROKE. (*Rising.*) Then run down to Freda and ask her to give you a clean slip. (MRS. ABBOT *rises.* GRACIE *moves up slightly.*) And remember— (GRACIE *stops.*) outside, Freda may be your friend; here she's your boss.

GRACIE. Yes. Mrs. Pembroke—I'll do everything she tells me to. (GRACIE *runs to the exit, then stops and comes quickly back, giving her mother a hasty kiss.*) Good-bye, mum.

MRS. ABBOT. Good-bye, my dear.

GRACIE. (*In a whisper.*) Leave the washin' up till I get home.

MRS. ABBOT. There'll be no need for that.

GRACIE. Good-bye! (*Running again to the exit.*)

MRS. PEMBROKE. Not too much noise, please! (*Rising.*)

GRACIE. Ever so sorry. (*Pulling herself up once again, her hand to her mouth, then going out more sedately.*)